PIZZA
CITY

Rivergate Regionals

Rivergate Regionals is a collection of books published by Rutgers University Press focusing on New Jersey and the surrounding area. Since its founding in 1936, Rutgers University Press has been devoted to serving the people of New Jersey and this collection solidifies that tradition. The books in the Rivergate Regionals Collection explore history, politics, nature and the environment, recreation, sports, health and medicine, and the arts. By incorporating the collection within the larger Rutgers University Press editorial program, the Rivergate Regionals Collection enhances our commitment to publishing the best books about our great state and the surrounding region.

PIZZA CITY

The Ultimate Guide to New York's Favorite Food

PETER GENOVESE

RUTGERS UNIVERSITY PRESS

New Brunswick, New Jersey, and London

Library of Congress Cataloging-in-Publication Data

Genovese, Peter, 1952–

Pizza city : the ultimate guide to New York's favorite food / Peter Genovese.

   p.   cm.

Includes bibliographical references and index.

ISBN 978–0–8135–5868–4 (pbk. : alk. paper)

ISBN 978–0–8135–5869–1 (e-book : alk. paper)

1. Restaurants—New York (State)—New York—Guidebooks. 2. New York (N.Y.)—Guidebooks. 3. Pizza.
  I. Title.

TX907.3.N72G45 2013

641.82'48—dc23   2012023494

A British Cataloging-in-Publication record for this book is available from the British Library.

Visit our website: http://rutgerspress.rutgers.edu

Manufactured in the United States of America

This book is dedicated to Kristin and Shirley, my pizza-eating pals, and the New York City subway system, without which this book would not have been possible.

Contents

Acknowledgments

Most of the interviews for this book were done by simply calling up or showing up, unannounced, at the pizzerias profiled. Not one owner told me to go away, or get lost, and for that I am grateful. Who said New Yorkers are not friendly and helpful?

Thanks to Louise "Cookie" Ciminieri, the inimitable co-owner of Totonno's, for sitting down one afternoon to tell me the history of the classic Coney Island pizzeria.

To Adam Kuban, who traced his love for pizza, and the beginning of *Slice*, at an Upper East Side pizzeria one night.

To Salvatore Natale, the irrepressible owner of Pugsley's, for his time and enthusiasm, and to his son, Pietro, for telling me his dad should be in the book!

To Paul Giannone, owner of Paulie Gee's, for the account of a Jersey guy who made his name in the big city.

To Agatha Mangano, the most determined woman in New York City, for talking about Ray's/Famous Ray's, and for allowing me to look at several boxes of photos, menus, and other memorabilia.

To Bob Alleva, owner of Alleva Dairy, for the stories of the country's oldest cheese store, especially the Great Cheese Heist.

To Joe Pozzuoli, the always-young owner of Joe's on Carmine, for the lowdown on the classic Village slice joint.

A sign of the times, Manhattan.

To Miki Agrawal, the dynamic owner of SLICE; wish I had half her energy.

To Scott Wiener, founder of Scott's Pizza Tours, for his inexhaustible pizza knowledge. Take a tour!

To Michael Frank, manager of John's on Bleecker, for his frank (couldn't help it!) discussion of the landmark pizzeria.

To Domenico DeMarco, owner of Di Fara's, for sitting down one rainy morning to talk about the legendary Brooklyn pizzeria.

To Palma Denino and her stepdaughter, Carla, and son, Michael, for their old-school warmth and friendliness, as befits Staten Island's best-known pizzeria.

To Jason Feirman, founder of the I Dream of Pizza blog, for his help, and for suggesting John's in Elmhurst as a subject.

To Chris Parachini, co-owner of Roberta's in Bushwick, who said he doesn't do interviews, but agreed to do one with me.

To Debbie Jones, manager of Eddie's Pizza Truck, and Mike Vallario, owner of Valducci's, for describing the ins and outs of the not-so-glamorous pizza truck business.

To John Brescia, co-owner of Lombardi's, for the history of the country's oldest pizzeria.

To Mark Bello, founder of Pizza a Casa, for letting me attend his pizza school, and for introducing me to Bob Alleva at Alleva Dairy.

To Mathieu Palombino, owner of Motorino, for taking the time in a tight schedule to discuss his West Village pizzeria.

To Shirley Chow, for opening up my eyes to the art and beauty of the lowly pizza box.

To Greg Barris, co-owner of L'Asso, for describing the joys and heartache of not only pizza making but also stand-up comedy.

To Rose and Susan Bagali, owners of John's in Elmhurst, for allowing me to hang out in their pizzeria all afternoon.

Finally, I've sung their praises before and I'm going to sing them again. It's been nearly ten years since I've worked with the wonderful folks at Rutgers University Press, and it was a joy to collaborate with them on *Pizza City*. Thanks first to Marlie Wasserman, the Press's director, for saying yes once again. Then Allyson Fields, her assistant; Marilyn Campbell, the prepress director; Anne Hegeman, the production manager; Ellen C. Dawson, the book designer and typesetter; and Elizabeth Scarpelli, the sales and marketing director. A writer is only as good as his copy editor, and India Cooper— a former New Yorker, she knows from pizza—did a terrific job with the manuscript. Hopefully it won't be another ten years before we all meet again.

PIZZA
CITY

Introduction

You may have seen me in your local pizzeria—bald-headed dude, huddled in the corner, eyeing the slices in front of him, sampling, evaluating, scribbling in a reporter's notebook, snapping off a few photos, dropping camera and notebook in messenger bag, pulling out a torn New York City subway map and walking out the door, on to the next stop.

There was always a next stop, always another interview, in the months I spent researching this book. There may have been more eating than interviewing and note taking, but from the beginning I decided that this book was not going to be simply a Zagat-like guide to New York City pizzerias, nor just a book about pizza in general.

It was going to be two pizza books in one—profiles of at least twenty pizza personalities (pizzeria owners, pizza bloggers, pizza tour operators, etc.), then honest reviews of as many pizzerias as I could visit (250, as it would turn out, with more than five hundred slices or pizzas sampled in all).

The idea of this book started to form after I completed a six-month journey into true pizza obsessiveness—the six months I spent leading a team of four pizza fanatics who

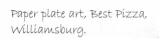

Paper plate art, Best Pizza, Williamsburg.

visited 350-plus pizzerias in New Jersey in a mission to rate and select the state's best pizzas for the Newark *Star-Ledger*, the newspaper I have been proud to call home for fifteen years. The project, known as the Pizza Patrol, resulted in a week-long series of stories in the *Star-Ledger* and a book titled *A Slice of Jersey*.

Ever on the hunt for book ideas, I wondered about New York City pizza. Surely someone had written a book focusing on the pizza scene in the world's greatest pizza city (sorry, Naples).

To my astonishment, no one had written that book.

Why?

Got me.

"Maybe it's just too challenging," someone suggested.

There have been thousands of newspaper and magazine stories over the years on pizza. There are hundreds—maybe thousands—of pizza blogs out there. Scores of documentaries on pizza. Dozens of pizza cookbooks. A handful of pizza history books.

Not one book strictly on New York City pizza.

Ed Levine, founder of seriouseats.com, wrote *Pizza: A Slice of Heaven* (Universe Publishing, 2009), an indispensable guide to the world of pizza. Ninety of its 368 pages are devoted to New York City.

Someone had to write the ultimate guide to pizza in the five boroughs.

Might as well be me.

I like challenges, even if the major one encountered in this book was not going into cardiac arrest from the constant onslaught of cheese.

From the beginning, the book was intended to be an account of one reporter's journey into the world of New York pizza. I love pizza—who doesn't?—but didn't want *Pizza City* to sound like Pizza Geek 101. It was not going to be filled with painfully detailed deconstructions of Neapolitan, New York–style, Sicilian, thin-crust, and all the other pizza styles out there. There is only one mention each of the word "cornicione" or "pizzaiola" in these pages. Pizzaiola?? For heaven's sake, they're pizza makers! Stop making pizza sound like a religion, or a cult, or a subject only a privileged few can join or fully "understand."

But I think you'll learn a lot in this book; I sure did. What kinds of cheese and tomatoes and ovens pizzerias use. Never-told-before stories involving places like Totonno's and Pugsley's and Denino's. Why Mike Frank at John's on Bleecker considers himself more "babysitter" than manager; how Chris Parachini, owner of Roberta's, and his pals built the renowned Bushwick restaurant brick by brick, or how Agatha Mangano, who oversees Famous Ray's and Famous Original Ray's, discovers pizzeria owners from as far away as Dublin are infringing on the company trademark.

Stories and details that, I hope, make this book come alive.

I wanted to go behind the scenes, dig deeper, tell stories previously not told. This required some doing. New

Sign, New Park Pizza, Howard Beach.

Yorkers are often portrayed as superior, snobbish. Pizza makers? Fiercely competitive and famously close-mouthed.

I expected doors to be shut in my face, phones to be hung up, e-mails to be ignored.

Boy, was I surprised. Not one person approached for an interview told me to go away. Everyone cooperated, even if a few required some sweet-talking, or arm-twisting.

The profiles are a mix of familiar names—Cookie Ciminieri at Totonno's and Domenic DeMarco at Di Fara's, among others—and lesser-known but no less captivating personalities, like Miki Agrawal, the owner of SLICE; Sal Natale, the lovably nutty proprietor of Pugsley's in the Bronx; and Rose and Susan Bagali, the mother-and-daughter team behind John's in Elmhurst, Queens.

Couldn't have done it without the New York City subway system.

I'm no stranger to food writing, or pizza obsession. My books include *Jersey Diners* and *The Food Lover's Guide to New Jersey*. I'm a feature writer at the *Star-Ledger* and write often about food for the state's largest newspaper.

I like pizza and wish there were more New York–quality pizzerias where I live, at the Jersey Shore. But Newark, where I work, is a ten-minute train ride to the big city, so great pizza is never far away.

(As far as which side of the river does pizza better, it's no contest; New York, New York.)

I went through countless MetroCards and saw more of the New York subway system than most New Yorkers do in their lifetime. Somehow my LDL did not rocket to dangerous levels. Or maybe it did, and I just didn't realize it.

In any event, this book was a lot of work and a lot of fun. If it opens your eyes to the great big pizza world out there, makes you suddenly crave a couple slices, or leads you to embark on your own sleepless search for the city's best pizza, well, then, I did my job.

Just don't blame me for your increased cholesterol level.

Pizza People

Pizza Conquers the World

Pizza is not a big business; it's an enormous, immense, colossal, vast, threatening-to-take-over-the-world business.

Wait, it's already taken over the world. The planet's most popular food dominates like no other item ever placed on a plate, paper or otherwise. In the United States alone, pizza is a $35 billion business—more than the gross national income of the United Arab Emirates. A slice replaced chicken nuggets as the preferred food of American schoolchildren years ago. There are a staggering 65,000 pizzerias across the country, about 1,600 in New York City alone.

No other food topic—maybe no other topic, period—gets New Yorkers going like pizza. For proof, check out Yelp, Yahoo, UrbanSpoon, and their counterparts, filled with swooningly ecstatic and devastatingly nasty reviews. God forbid you call out someone else's favorite pizzeria.

A marriage made in heaven, Greenpoint.

"You can't walk down the streets of this city and not talk about pizza," says Scott Wiener, who runs Scott's Pizza Tours and knows as much about New York pizza as any person alive.

There are annual pizza conventions in Las Vegas and New York City. Pizza Hut, which controls 12 percent of the U.S. pizza market (Domino's has 8 percent), has restaurants in scores of countries, including Bahrain (eleven), Honduras (eight), Thailand (seventy-five), and Malaysia, where you can get the usual Pizza Hut standards plus the Golden Fortune Cheesy Crown pizza, topped with deep-fried fish, shrimp, and pineapple.

Top five pizza sales days
  Super Bowl Sunday
  New Year's Eve
  Halloween
  The night before Thanksgiving
  New Year's Day

Disclosure: the last time I visited Pizza Hut was in Bangkok. It will come as no surprise to anyone that it tasted just like the one in Dubuque and Denver and Dallas. There are more than 250 Pizza Huts in nearly sixty Indian cities; the Pizza Hut India website describes PH as "India's most trusted restaurant brand."

Domino's, the Avis to Pizza Hut's Hertz, has more than six hundred locations in India. The pizza boom in Southeast Asia and Europe especially is so dramatic that it's only a matter of time before Domino's sells more pizzas overseas than in the United States, and Domino's rang up $3.5 billion in pizza sales in this country last year. By the way, Domino's sells more pizza per capita in Iceland than in any other country.

"The numbers show an industry that is fighting back from a recession—and is on its way to winning," *PMQ Pizza Magazine* reported in its latest Pizza Power Report. How did pizza achieve global dominance? Blame it on the Greeks. Or Romans. Or Egyptians. Or whoever first put flatbread with some sort of topping (we're not talking bufala mozzarella or sun-dried tomatoes here) over a heat source.

Pizza as we know it today, though, begins in Italy, specifically Naples, where pizza was a popular food for the city's poor from the eighteenth century on. Everyone seemed to hate pizza outside of Naples. Northern Italians turned up their noses. Samuel Morse, inventor of the telegraph, described pizza, which he sampled on a visit in 1831, as "a species of most nauseating cake" resembling a piece of bread "that had been taken reeking out of the sewer."

Wonder what Sam would have thought of pizza today?

While the rest of Italy ignored or even detested pizza, Neapolitans couldn't get enough of it. When Queen Margherita, wife of King Umberto I, declared a pizza with mozzarella, tomatoes, and basil her favorite on a visit to Naples in 1889, pizza received a stamp of approval it would never relinquish.

Top ten pizza chains by number of units
(*PMQ Pizza Magazine*)

1	Pizza Hut
2	Domino's Pizza
3	Papa John's
4	Little Caesars
5	Papa Murphy's Take 'N' Bake Pizza
6	Sbarro
7	Godfather's Pizza
8	CiCi's Pizza
9	Hungry Howie's Pizza & Subs
10	Chuck E. Cheese

It wasn't until after World War II that pizza became widely popular, first in Italy, then America, then the rest of the world. Much has been made of American GIs returning home after the war craving the dish they had fallen in love with in Italy. In fact, as Carol Helstosky, author of *Pizza: A Global History* (about as succinct a history of a food as you'll find anywhere), says, the seeds had already been planted by southern Italians moving to northern Italy and then the rest of Europe and bringing their eating habits with them. Pizzerias popped up everywhere from Milan to Stockholm. Pizza's global march was under way.

Pizza came to America in the late 1800s with Italian immigrants like Gennaro Lombardi, who acquired the first mercantile license to sell pizza in this country and opened a grocery/pizza store on Spring Street in New York in 1905. Nearly one-third of Italy's population emigrated to the United States between 1876 and 1924, and they brought their foods and recipes with them. Lombardi's became the center of what would become known as Little Italy, and the training ground for such pizza makers as Anthony Pero, who opened Totonno's in 1924, and John Sasso, who opened John's in 1929.

Pizza spread through Italian neighborhoods in New Jersey, Boston, and New Haven, where Frank Pepe sold a white pizza with olive oil, oregano, and anchovies from a street cart before opening Pepe's in 1925.

A year later, Pizzeria Regina opened in Boston. In 1933, Patsy's opened in East Harlem; in 1934, Sciortino's had its start in Perth Amboy. By the time the GIs returned home after World War II, pizza was already waiting for them.

In 1943, Pizzeria Uno launched in Chicago; hello, deep-dish pizza. In 1957, Celentano Brothers released the first supermarket frozen pizza, a year before Frank and Dan Carney, students at the University of Wichita (now Wichita State University), opened Pizza Hut in a converted bar next to the family grocery store.

The words of the prophet are written on the subway walls . . .

States with the most pizza stores per 10,000 people (*PMQ Pizza Magazine*)		States with the fewest pizza stores per 10,000 people (*PMQ Pizza Magazine*)	
1 Massachusetts	6 Pennsylvania	1 Arkansas	6 California
2 New Hampshire	7 Maine	2 Tennessee	7 South Carolina
3 Connecticut	8 New Jersey	3 Oklahoma	8 Arizona
4 Iowa	9 Delaware	4 North Carolina	9 New Mexico
5 Rhode Island	10 Ohio	5 Washington	10 Utah
(New York is 11th)			

In 1959, the first Little Caesars opened. In 1967, Domino's, which began as Dominick's in 1960, opened its first store, in Ypsilanti, Michigan.

Dying to know about Tombstone Pizza? In 1962, Pep Simek, who with his brother ran a bar next to a cemetery in Medford, Wisconsin, broke his leg dancing. He spent most of the winter tinkering with pizza recipes for bar patrons. That's how Tombstone Pizza was born.

Choking posters, required in all restaurants.

The first Papa John's (now the third-largest pizza chain after Pizza Hut and Domino's) opened in 1984; Kraft, which purchased Tombstone Pizza in 1986, introduced DiGiorno, with its revolutionary "self-rising" crust.

New York magazine offered a different kind of pizza timeline in a 2009 issue. The period from 1664 to 1889 is labeled "The Dark Ages—a pre-pizza New York." The average cost of a slice in 1956 was 15 cents, a price that kept pace "with the cost of subway fare, seen as a kind of an economic indicator." Levy's on Pitkin Avenue in East New York, according to the timeline, introduced the first kosher pizza in 1958, and in 1964, Robert F. Kennedy reportedly asked for a fork when offered a pizza on the campaign trail (aides denied the story). In 1984, the *Journal of the American Dental Association* coined the term "pizza palate" to describe "a burned and ulcerated roof of the mouth, the bane of overanxious pizza eaters." In 1987, the Quilted Giraffe started serving tuna sashimi-and-wasabi pizza, while 2004 saw the "dawn of a new regime," with Una Pizza Napoletano (since closed) and Franny's serving Naples-style pizzas, unsliced.

No matter how you tell its history, it's clear that pizza rules the world. You can find pizza everywhere from Elmhurst to Ulan Bator to Uzbekistan. (Layover in Tashkent? There's pizza at Pizza New World, Moskovskaya Pizza, and Super Duper.)

New York City? With 1,600 pizzerias, it's the center of the pizza universe. The latest moves, trends, and developments in the business are analyzed with the attention usually reserved for unemployment numbers or the collapse of foreign governments. In 1998, a *New York Times* headline announced, "New York Pizza, the Real Thing, Makes a Comeback," a reference to the quick-cooked, quality-mozzarella-topped pizzas, usually from coal-fired ovens, emerging at places like Grimaldi's, Lombardi's (which had reopened after being closed for ten years), Nick's in Forest Hills, and elsewhere.

In 2009, the *Times* discovered that "indiscriminate gluttons and discerning gourmands alike" had "elevated their passion to a vocation, sending pizza into a whole new stratosphere of respect. It isn't just loved, and it isn't just devoured. It's scrutinized and fetishized, with a Palin-esque power to polarize."

A year later, the *Times* announced that pizza had entered "a golden age," with "blistered, bubbling" Naples-style pizza, "once a hard-to-find pleasure," now "almost routine." Today, everyone seems to want in on pizza in New York City, from corner delis to high-end restaurants. Even the big pizza chains realize they need to stay ahead of ever-changing pizza tastes and trends. In 2011, Domino's introduced "Artisan Pizza," with such choices as Tuscan salami and roasted vegetables, spinach and feta, and Italian sausage and pepper. The takeout boxes are even signed by the person who made the pizza. And Papa John's started offering dollar slices at four locations in the city, a development other chains will no doubt follow.

Styles of pizza as identified by *Pizza Today* magazine

1 Neapolitan: cooked in wood-burning ovens, feature "charred crust, spare topping, and a raised border."

2 Sicilian: baked in rectangular pan and cut into squares.

3 Roman: thin crust, oblong shape.

4 New York: "the most imitated style of pizza in the United States," characterized by "oversized, foldable slices that can be eaten on the go."

5 New Haven: thin, crispy, oval-shaped.

6 Tomato Trenton: sauce goes on top of cheese.

7 Chicago thick: stuffed deep-dish; hearty, filling.

8 Chicago thin: crispy, thin-crusted, often cut into squares; also known as "tavern pizza."

9 Traditional American: based on New York–style pizza, but generally a bit thicker and uses more cheese.

10 Deep-dish: as opposed to Chicago thick or stuffed pizza, all toppings placed on top.

11 California artisan: uses a variety of toppings and ingredients; emphasis on freshness and creativity.

12 Grandma: a thin-crust Sicilian popular on Long Island

13 Grilled pizza: a specialty of Providence, Rhode Island.

14 St. Louis: cheese is a blend of Swiss, provolone, and white cheddar.

Every day, there seem to be a new development, a new twist, in this $35 billion business. You don't have to look any farther than New York. Pizza fanatics mourned when Ray's Pizza on Prince Street closed for good in October 2011 but rejoiced several weeks later when Patsy Grimaldi, one of the legendary New York pizza names, announced he was coming out of retirement to run Grimaldi's Old Fulton Street location, which would be named Juliana's, after his late mother. The Old Fulton Street location had been run by Frank Ciolli, who had been delinquent in rent and then lost his lease. Ciolli relocated Grimaldi's—next door to Patsy's new place.

A Pizza Timeline (from various sources)

1830   The earliest known pizzeria, Antica Pizzeria Port'Alba, opens in Naples.

1905   Lombardi's on Spring Street in New York City is issued America's first mercantile license to bake pizza.

1910   Joe's Tomato Pies opens in the Chambersburg section of Trenton, N.J.

1912   Papa's Tomato Pies opens, also in Trenton. Unlike Joe's, it is still open.

1924   Anthony "Totonno" Pero opens Totonno's Pizzeria in Coney Island, N.Y.

1925   Frank Pepe opens Frank Pepe Pizzeria Napoletana in New Haven, Conn.

1926   Pizzeria Regina opens in Boston.

1929   John Sasso opens John's Pizzeria in Greenwich Village.

1929   Marra's opens in Philadelphia.

1933   Patsy's opens in East Harlem.

1934   Sciortino's begins business in Perth Amboy, N.J. (it is now located in South Amboy).

1936   The Reservoir Tavern opens in Parsippany, N.J.

1957   Celentano Brothers releases the first supermarket frozen pizza.

1958   Frank and Dan Carney, students at the University of Wichita (now Wichita State University) open Pizza Hut in a converted bar next to the family grocery store. Two years later, there are 25 Pizza Huts. By 1977, Pizza Hut is a billion-dollar-a-year company with 3,400 stores worldwide.

1959   The first Little Caesars opens.

1962   Pep Simek, who with his brother runs a bar bordered by a cemetery in Medford, Wisc., breaks his leg dancing and spends most of the winter tinkering with pizza recipes for bar patrons. Tombstone Pizza is born.

1967   The first Domino's opens.

1984   The first Papa John's opens.

1995   Kraft, which had purchased Tombstone in 1986, unveils DiGiorno and its revolutionary "self-rising" crust.

Talk about Pizza Wars.

Pizza—the food, the business, the culture, the phenomenon—shows no signs of slowing its gooey global march. It's only a matter of time before pizza reaches Antarctica.

Wait, it's already in Antarctica. There's a Pizza Hut Antarctica Facebook page, but it's a lark, likely the work of scientists with too much time on their hands, advertising such specials as "anchovie and seal pizza" and "penguin wings."

This is real, though: at the Australian Antarctic research station on Casey, Windmill Islands, pizza is a menu staple. From the photos on the station's website, it looks pretty tasty.

Totonno's

When asked her age, the co-owner of Coney Island's most famous pizzeria fixes you with a stare that would stop the Cyclone in its tracks.

"Come over here, look at this," says Louise Ciminieri, pointing to a photo of Gennaro Lombardi and her grandfather Anthony Pero on the wall at Totonno's on Coney Island.

Louise "Cookie" Ciminieri, co-owner of Totonno's on Coney Island.

Anthony Pero, founder of Totonno's.

Pero worked at Lombardi's before opening Totonno's in the early 1920s. The same photo is on the wall at Lombardi's.

The woman everyone calls "Cookie" wants to make sure you realize something about Lombardi's, acknowledged as New York's—and the country's—first pizzeria. Cookie points to Gennaro Lombardi's shiny black dress shoes. "This is not a pizza maker," she says dismissively. Then she points to her grandfather's flour-dusted shoes. "This is a pizza maker. My grandfather was born in Naples. He worked for Lombardi's making pizza. His pizza. My grandfather created pizza in this country."

A bold, even outrageous, statement, but you want to argue with this woman?

"Today, it's original this, original that." Cookie continues. "We're the original, we're the only ones. Zagat named us [New York's] number one [pizzeria] in 2012. Number two, I never heard of."

Totonno's. The name is synonymous with Coney Island, right there with the Cyclone and Wonder Wheel. Totonno's, after Pero's first name, opened in its current location, on Neptune Avenue, in 1924, but Cookie says it actually started across the street. When?

Can of imported olive oil, Totonno's.

Lettering, Totonno's.

Get a slice of history
on the walls at Totonno's.

"I don't know. Everybody's dead. They just told me here in 1924."

As a kid she heard the "cowboys" singing country-western music in a theater on the boardwalk. "All the way over here you could hear them," she says wistfully.

The pizzeria's exterior and interior seem frozen in time—"Totonno's" in classic gray stenciled letters on the window, the walls covered with photos of everyone from Babe Ruth to George W. Bush. Look, there's Willie Mays, and the 1955 world champion Brooklyn Dodgers. "Truman Announces War Over," proclaims a newspaper headline. The "most amazing" photo of all, according to Cookie, is one of Joe DiMaggio signing a ball for John F. Kennedy—at Fenway Park.

"People ask me, 'When are you going to put up the Mets?'" She smiles. "When they earn it."

It is late afternoon, and quiet. There are just two customers, guys in their forties about to settle their bill.

Late afternoon,
Totonno's, Coney Island.

"I got it," says one.

"No, I got it."

"I told you I got it."

"Soze," says the other, dropping money on the table. "I told you I got it."

Soze mentions Joe and Pat's on Staten Island. That gets Cookie going. The Food Network wanted to host a pizza showdown between Totonno's and Joe and Pat's. Cookie put the kibosh on that.

"They wanted me to defend my pizza against them," she says. "I don't have to do nothing. Listen to me"—it is one of her trademark phrases—"I live on Staten Island. There are six [restaurants] on Staten Island I'll eat at."

There's always been a coal-fired oven at Totonno's, and it's whole pies only; don't you dare ask for a slice.

"We have one thing most people don't have—a recipe," Cookie continues. "Most people who open [a pizzeria] these days go to a trade magazine, which tells them what to do. The difference is that no one uses the ingredients we do," she adds. "No one uses my dough. We buy the cheese from someone no one else uses."

Behind the curtain is . . . the bathroom.

You want to argue with this woman, go right ahead.

The most popular pizza at Totonno's is a toss-up between the white and the margherita. The pizzeria is normally closed Mondays and Tuesdays, except in the summer, when the Brooklyn Cyclones play. There's a pizzeria inside the stadium, but Cyclones staff will regularly call Totonno's and order ten pizzas at a time.

The restroom is hidden behind a curtain to the left of the counter. The 1939 radio against the wall is her grandmother's.

Cookie started working here in 1975; one day her Aunt Julia told her to take care of one half of the dining room, and that was that. "From this side I went to the other side, and then I started running the whole shebang," Cookie says.

Her grandfather, who was fond of silk shirts and loved the opera, worked at the pizzeria until the early 1950s; then her Uncle Jerry took over. "They weren't making that many pizzas. They weren't open that many hours. They'd open at 2:30, close maybe 6."

One day, Uncle Jerry got sick and she was pressed into emergency pizza-making duty. "He fell to the side, got dizzy. He said, 'You make the pies.'

The line was way outside. I used to watch him; I knew what to do."

How old was she then?

Wrong question.

"There you are again with the 'how old.' I was making the pizza, OK?"

Her husband, Joel, made pizzas for years. He was known for his imitations—"he did Jackie Mason better than Jackie Mason," according to Cookie. Uncle Jerry passed away and Joel got sick, so their son, Lawrence, a former food and beverage manager at Caesars in Vegas, started working at Totonno's. "We threw him in the kitchen, started him on the prep work. Then my husband passed away. All these people died on me."

Totonno's, circa 1940.

Has anything at Totonno's changed over the years?

"We haven't changed anything. We use the same recipe. Look around. Does it look like we changed anything?"

Cookie may seem gruff at first, and an early Zagat review likened the service to what you'd get from "the Marquis de Sade," but Cookie's a sweetheart—once she gets to know you.

Steven A. Shaw, co-founder of *eGullet,* said in his *Fat Guy Guide to Pizza* (a kind of underground pizza classic, written in stages around 2000) that the pizza at Totonno's had not only declined over the years but that "it simply isn't even all that good anymore." At the time, Shaw said Totonno's owners, who "appear on television and make the outrageous claim that nothing has changed," should be "hauled into the public square, pilloried and mercilessly pelted with the same overripe, metallic-tasting tomatoes that form the basis of their present-day sauce."

Apparently, things have changed between now and then, because the pizza on my visit tasted just fine. Pizza debates—about Totonno's, about any New York pizzeria—are always good, though.

Totonno's was damaged by a fire in March 2009 that started in the oven firebox. The pizzeria was forced to close down for eleven months; regulars were distraught. The furniture was refinished. But not replaced.

As if to cement Totonno's standing in the New York pizza firmament, Mayor Michael Bloomberg was on hand to cut the ribbon at the pizzeria's reopening in July 2011. Cookie, her sister Antoinette, and her brother Frank are the co-owners. There were once

Vinnie Amato,
pizza maker, Totonno's.

two Totonno's in Manhattan and one in Yonkers. They have since closed. Why? "The leases were up," Cookie says. "The landlords." She pauses. "We don't need to go there."

There's a Facebook page, but that's as modern as this place gets.

"I will not have a fax machine," Cookie says. "No computer. No e-mail. We have a telephone, one line. People ask, 'Why do you sell just pizza?' We don't know anything about any other food except pizza."

The Founder of *Slice*

The guy sitting at the window table at San Matteo Panuozzo on the Upper East Side doesn't look like a pizza obsessive.

With his beard and owlish glasses, Adam Kuban looks more like a grad student, or a professor at some small college in the Midwest, where he's from.

Kuban may cringe at the word "obsessive"—his posts on the *Slice* pizza blog are refreshingly free of posturing and pizza tech talk—but it is the word, after all, he used in a headline on a self-interview for *Slice*.

Adam Kuban, founder of *Slice*, the country's leading pizza blog.

"One of my other interviews fell through, and I needed someone quick to fill the slot," he explained at the time.

No one covers the New York pizza scene like he does. Or *Slice*. Founded by Kuban in 2003, *Slice* is the city's—the nation's—number-one pizza blog. It's where you go for the latest breaking pizza news, and for reviews by Kuban and others on pizzerias in New York and beyond.

January 21, 2011

Pizza by CerTé, where have I been all your life? Yeah, I know all the bloggers have been singing your praises since you opened last year in April—notably Midtown Lunch's Brownie, who comes close to calling it the best slice in Midtown. Despite all that, yesterday was my first time visiting—can you believe that? Billed as a "baker's" pizza on the menu, it's somewhere between a Grandma and a Sicilian pizza, with more rise and sponginess to it than the former but not the often overwhelming volume of the latter. And it has just the right crunch-to-chew ratio. I'm kicking myself for sleeping on this slice.

Kuban was born in Cudahy, Wisconsin, which he calls "the Staten Island of Milwaukee," a pretty good line for those of us who attended college in Beer Town.

Kuban's dad sold cemetery plots—still does.

"He's always been kind of entrepreneurial," Kuban says, smiling.

17

Kuban, center, was making pizzas at an early age.

His dad's company kept relocating him around the country, and the family moved with him—a year in Richmond; a year in Bradford, Pennsylvania; a year in Denver; a year in Duluth. Kuban doesn't remember his first slice, but his first pizza was the Milwaukee-style one he and his dad would make at home, which was then outside Boston. His dad always wanted to open his own pizzeria, which he did in Olathe, Kansas. Mamma Mia's lasted a year and half; a Pizza Hut had opened nearby, but Kuban isn't sure Mamma Mia's would have lasted anyway. His fondest memory of the place is playing video games with the blue quarters his dad gave him for sweeping and other duties.

A self-described "huge photography nerd" in high school, Kuban majored in journalism at Kansas. He served as writer and copy editor for the university paper—"I always had this need to communicate, to tell stories"—and started a zine called *Big Time Pinball*. It lasted exactly one issue.

Dad talked him into trying pharmacy as a career, so Kuban enrolled in the pre-pharmacy program at Kansas. He promptly got a D in organic chemistry. After graduation, he moved to Oregon and worked as a newspaper copy editor. In Salem, he thought about starting a pizza zine, which he would call *Pizza Blast*. In a minimalist mood, he changed his mind and came up with the name *Slice*. But that's as far as it went.

He moved to Portland, then to New York in 2000. In 2003, *Gothamist* and other city-centric blogs were just getting off the ground. "This is cool," Kuban thought at the time. "I want one."

Which resulted in *Hatchback* ("I owned one or two"), but the blog didn't have anything to do with pizza.

"It was stupid stuff, nothing worthy," he says, grimacing.

In New York, he worked as a copy editor at *Martha Stewart Living* magazine. And like any true New Yorker, he started taking his pizza seriously.

"In my personal mythology," he says, "I like to say I was eating a slice a day. After a while I got sick of pizza. That led me to the discovery not all pizza was great. I thought, 'There's got to be a fan page for pizza; there's a fan page for everything else.'"

Slice started in 2003 as an aggregator, linking to posts by Ed Levine (author of *A Slice of Heaven* and founder of *Serious Eats*), the *Village Voice's* Robert Sietsema, and others. Kuban's first review, of Nunzio's on Staten Island, appeared November 7, 2003:

> We had ordered one plain regular and one plain Sicilian each. Why we ordered Sicilian is beyond me. Actually, I was starving by the time we arrived, and the thick, square slice was especially appealing. At table, the slices looked great. Islands of mozzarella floating on a bed of sauce promised the proper balance of a slice's, or a pie's, essential trio of ingredients: dough, sauce, cheese. . . .
>
> My first bite yielded an almost grilled cheese–like taste: a mouthful of cheese with a hint of overdoneness. This is unfortunate because the sauce is quite tasty. Bright and fresh, it is made with San Marzano tomatoes, the Italian imports favored for sauces because of their meatiness and less-acidic taste. If only the cheese didn't mask it.

Slice was not an immediate hit. Then *Law & Order* stepped in. Kuban was watching an episode filmed, he realized, in Grimaldi's. He e-mailed Jen Chung, co-founder of *Gothamist*, who mentioned *Slice* in a post. *Gawker*, the news and gossip sheet, did likewise. *Slice* had been noticed.

Kuban estimates there were about two hundred food-oriented blogs in the English-speaking world when he started *Slice*, but says the blog was "the first single-topic niche site for food." At the start, he tried to post something daily; actual reviews appeared every two or three weeks. "From the beginning, I was always conscious about not marginalizing the other boroughs—no cheap shots at Staten Island or Queens."

> June 17, 2011
>
> How 'bout the weather lately, right? Not too hot, not too cold. Not humid. Perfect for pizza under the stars. Taking my own advice from earlier this year (9 NYC Pizzerias with Great Gardens), I made my way to Saraghina in Bed-Stuy to catch up on things. First, what I love about Saraghina: the garden. . . . I like the pizza, too, but I don't love it. On a recent night, our party of four sampled a trio of pies and found them a little wanting. The crust, though crisp and chewy and moderately puffy at the rim, could have used more salt, more flavor. Once past the smokiness of the more well-done parts of the *cornicione* (what Italians call the edge of the pizza), there was very little we tasted beyond a sort of white-bread inoffensiveness.

Kuban had become a voice, and force, to be reckoned with. The owner of Fornino in Brooklyn put Kuban's photo on the wall and told his staff to let him know if that guy showed up.

FACT:
Pizza is the number-one search word on Google. The top three restaurants searched on Google are Pizza Hut, Domino's, and Papa John's.

Slice attracted fans, followers, self-described "pizza nerds," and more than a few zealots. "Every once in a while the [Neapolitan pizza] diehards come on. I think I scared them off." He smiles. "They're such blowhards. There have been some haters. They've moved on."

October 22, 2008

> It's been little things building. Hangovers after two beers, increasing instances of heartburn, a newfound appreciation for Billy Joel. But I think I officially became old on Monday when I admitted I was scared of teenagers.
>
> But, so far, only when I'm carrying pizza on the subway.
>
> Returning from Motorino on Monday with a Margherita pizza for the office, I was traveling by subway just as school let out. Boisterous clusters of teenagers roamed the streets and gathered on the subway platforms belowground.
>
> And all I could think of was how one of these kids might start something with me—demanding a slice or simply knocking the box from below, lunch-tray-bully style.

Along the way, Kuban founded the blog *A Hamburger Today* (burgers are a close second to pizza as his favorite food) and was the founding editor at *Serious Eats*. In 2006, he sold *Slice* and *A Hamburger Today* to *Serious Eats*. At the time, he was making "a couple hundred bucks a month" on Google ads.

"It didn't make me a millionaire. Maybe a thousandaire. I had some credit card debt at the time; it took care of that."

In 2010, he got married—his wife is known online as "Girl Slice." He left *Serious Eats* for good in May 2011, although he still writes weekly pieces, plus a monthly column on cooking at home.

"I've been kind of diluted to the point where people don't realize I founded this thing and was writing about pizza for eight years," he says of *Slice*.

His "desert island" or "last meal" pizza would be a midwestern-style thin crust "with a good, freshly made chunky fennel sausage topping."

Sausage and red onions are the Astoria resident's favorite toppings. He would never put seafood, apart from clams or anchovies, on a pizza.

He wishes people would stop taking pizza so seriously, which seems an impossible task in New York City.

"The biggest thing I'd like to say is that PEOPLE, IT'S JUST PIZZA," he wrote in his "self-interview." "That's not to say it's not important, but I just don't get all the purist stuff, all the stridency, all the my-(pie)-way-or-the-highway attitude. Thankfully, *Slice* has

"Without question, the greatest invention in the history of mankind is beer. Oh, I grant you that the wheel was also a fine invention, but the wheel does not go nearly as well with pizza."
—Dave Barry

enjoyed a long period of relative calm in the comments section, but whenever discussion devolves into sniping, I'm just like WTF, *Slice*'rs?!? This is pizza, fercryinoutloud!"

"I've written everything I can say about pizza," he says toward the end of our conversation at San Matteo.

The *Slice* faithful will disagree.

When the self-interview on *Slice* appeared, they were quick to pay him tribute.

"A great interview OF the Slicemeister BY the Slicemeister!" dmcavanauch wrote. "You rule the pizza world, thanks for all the entertainment and pizza obsessiveness you provide all of us. The influence you and SLICE have had on the home making pizza community can be seen every Monday right here on MPM. Love my visits here, can't wait to meet you in person and hope we can share a slice or two while we're at it. Now about that "PEOPLE, IT'S JUST PIZZA" statement, you know better than that! It's NEVER just PIZZA. :-)"

A poster named famdoc said his childhood love of New York pizza was "reawakened" due to Kuban and *Slice*.

"Adam, both through his writing and through his personal charisma, was a big influence on me, and, I am sure, many others, in this way," famdoc said. "Now, Adam is a big shot. He travels the world, he is quoted in the press, his reviews appear in the windows of pizza joints around the world. Yet, he's never too busy to answer my e-mails, to guide me along the path of pizza perfection, to even quote me on rare occasions.

"Nice interview. Nice man. My grandmother would call him a mensch."

Wait for the Rainbow It Will Decorate the Sky

If you ranked the boroughs by quality of pizza, the Bronx would end up last. Even Staten Island, the "forgotten" borough, ends up higher on everyone's list.

But neither Brooklyn, Manhattan, Queens, nor Staten Island boasts a pizzeria quite like Pugsley's Pizza, on East 191st Street, right outside the gates to Fordham University. Nor an owner quite like Sal Natale.

Salvatore Natale, co-owner of Pugsley's Pizza, the Bronx.

A replica of the Statue of Liberty is one of many decorative touches inside Pugsley's.

The sax-playing, tai-chi-practicing, boyish Natale—sixty-seven going on seventeen—is the star attraction at Pugsley's, whose transformation from former stable and junkyard to Fordham's coolest hangout is an unlikely as the coming-to-America story of its owner.

Pugsley's is a museum of kitsch, tiki bar meets pizzeria by way of Dr. Seuss or Dr. Demento. There are four wood-beamed booths, one for each season. An eight-foot-high Statue of Liberty; a paper plate taped to its front reads, "Do not underestimate the power of the woman." A table in the corner, next to the door leading to the basement and the bathrooms, is made from a piece of sidewalk.

A message scrawled on a smiley-face-decorated piece of paper says, "If you're not in a good mood, then change it!"

Written in Italian above the booths: "A flower needs water and sunshine, the heart needs affection and love."

A sign at the far right counter: "Do not order here. The person here is only available to make delicious food and to bull—— with people."

"My name is Salvatore Natale," the chief BS-er says at the start, as if this is a job interview. "I come from Sicily. She" —he looks at his wife, Pina— "is the boss. I'm the troublemaker."

An inspirational message, of sorts, at Pugsley's.

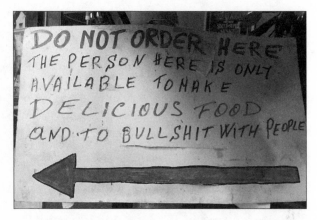

Rule number one at Pugsley's: Don't take any of the signs too seriously.

He was born in Sicily, in the town of Santa Caterina Villarmosa, a province of Caltanissetta.

"My father was a farmer; we lived in the town," Natale says. "We grew wheat, had a couple cows, a donkey, horse, chicken, couple rabbits."

He was a "beautiful" kid—but of course—who worked as an apprentice at a local blacksmith's. The town had a sixty-piece band, and he wanted to play in it. He told his teacher his dream; his teacher told him to go home.

The precocious one would eventually form his own band to play at weddings and other occasions. "Boys would pay us with [food] to serenade their girlfriends."

Still in his teens, he made windows and doors. But his mind and heart were on the music, always the music. He spots a saxophone in a storefront window and wants it more than anything he's ever wanted. But he can't afford it.

"I'm hot, I have money for cigarettes, everything, but still I am not happy. I wanted the saxophone."

His parents allow him to go to Germany to find a better job; Natale ends up on the assembly line at a Volkswagen plant. He buys a "cheap" saxophone, then a good one, and plays in a "rock and roll" band called Rooster. His father files papers to send him to America, and at the age of twenty-two, Sal Natale lands in New York City, where his uncle finds him a job at a body shop. Sal later makes furniture and forms a band called the Crazy Hearts.

"The hottest Italian band in New York," he says. "All the big Italian singers would come from Italy, we'd play before them, we'd kick their ass." He smiles. "I go onstage, I am hot, I am crazy."

"There's no better feeling in the world than a warm pizza on your lap."
—Kevin James

23

One of many whimsical messages at Pugsley's.

Hang in there, this story gets to pizza in a minute.

A friend introduces Sal to the president of the local ironworkers union, and Sal meets a worker named Sam who's been at the same job for twenty years. Sal doesn't want to end up like him, so he quits his job the next day. The drummer in Crazy Hearts works at a pizzeria on Pugsley Avenue in Bronx's Dorchester section. What's it called? Pugsley's, what else? Sal eventually buys out the owner and reopens Pugsley's at East 194th Street and Briggs Avenue. The store is later destroyed in a fire, so he scouts for a location closer to Fordham University. He spots a gas station on Fordham Road; the owner says it's not for sale but tells Natale about the vacant space out back.

At the time, the former stable is a pile of rubble and garbage, and Natale almost single-handedly transforms it into a pizzeria, which opens in 1985.

The exterior of Pugsley's provides no clue to the wonderland of kitsch inside.

Six months later, he opens a downstairs bar where the waitresses wear tight black outfits with devil's horns and tails; upstairs, the waitresses wear white angel outfits with wings. He later opens a jazz club downstairs; you can still spot "Jazz" formed in wrought iron on the back alley door.

Natale's plan was to stay open for a year, then "get out." So what happened?

"I made a lot of money," he says with a laugh. "We were making music, we were making money, we were making pizza, we were making kids happy."

He asks a cousin about Pina—the two had grown up in the same village in Sicily—wondering if she is "available." The two dance at a wedding; later they get engaged. Natale returns to the United States, while Pina stays in Sicily. He writes a song called "Thinking of You," tapes it, and calls her up, placing the tape recorder in his dough mixer bowl so she can hear it better. Pina cannot resist the crazy man's attention.

The two, who now have three daughters and one son, make quite a team behind the counter—Sal bouncy and buoyant, Pina quieter, more assured, rolling her eyes when her husband says something silly.

Pugsley's is not your average pizzeria, decor-wise.

He says his sauce is partly based on suggestions from a former cook at Mama Leone's. "She said, get good tomatoes, a little bit of salt, a little bit of pepper, a little bit of sugar, a little bit of oregano, and lots of passion and love."

"That last part was what she said?"

"No, that's what I said."

The pizzeria is tucked into a residential block—look for the large red "Pizza" sign and the patio with mismatched furniture. There's a reclining chair just inside the entrance, a long counter with stools, the four wooden booths, and a corner nook just past Miss Liberty. A wooden sculpture in the shape of the number 1 represents his wife; the four stones at the base, his kids.

One message is a reminder of Hurricane Gloria in 1985.

Under the red exit sign is the pizzeria's motto—"Love is it!"

A mural on the far wall is a reminder of Hurricane Gloria in 1985— "Do not fear the storm it will go by" and "Wait for the rainbow it will decorate the sky."

Sal plays the sax on occasion—you'll find clips on YouTube—and rings the big brass gong behind the counter when someone orders a pizza.

There are frequent karaoke events and costume parties and other merry mayhem. A photo on Pugsley's Facebook page shows Sal, who will apparently do anything, with an upturned bucket overflowing with spaghetti atop his head.

"Pugsley's! I had a dream about you last night!" screams one Facebook fan.

The crazy one does his tai chi before coming to work; he learned it from an instructor who told him he had to show up at 6:30 every morning and there would only be one excuse for missing class—a funeral. His own.

Asked how he lives his life, Pugsley's proprietor takes a moment to respond.

"Follow your heart. Do not let anyone steal your dream. If you have a song to sing, sing it. If you have a bell to ring, ring it. If you have a story to tell, tell it."

And how would he describe himself?

"Philosopher. Poet. Romantic. Musician. Pizza man. Bull— artist. Playboy."

Still?

Big laugh. "I'm out of practice."

Paulie Gee

Those who think social media are overrated should listen to the story of the sixties-rock-music-loving proprietor of the pizzeria hidden behind the massive doors of a former firehouse in Brooklyn.

When Paul Giannone opened his restaurant in March 2010, few knew his last name—he was just "Paulie Gee," some guy from Jersey. But everyone in New York, it seemed, knew about his pizzeria; the blogosphere had been abuzz for months about a hot new Brooklyn pizzeria—not in Williamsburg, not in South Slope, but . . . Greenpoint? The neighborhood of Polish delis, markets, and travel agencies somehow seemed a perfect fit for Giannone. He wanted to distance himself from the glitter and glam elsewhere. Not to mention it was considerably cheaper.

Paul Giannone, owner of
Paulie Gee's in Greenpoint.

So how did Giannone drum up interest in the already oversaturated New York City pizza market?

Networking, with a healthy dose of Internet. Smart Move Number One: He invites influential New York City pizza personalities like Adam Kuban (*Slice*) and Scott Wiener (Scott's Pizza Tours) to a pizza party at his house in Central Jersey. Rave reviews immediately appear online. Paulie tweets that he has just received his oven. On Facebook, he informs everyone the opening is weeks away. By the time the pizzeria opened in March 2010, anticipation was high. "Congrats to Paulie," Casey from San Francisco posted the morning after the opening. "He's redefining pizza in the boroughs. Looking forward to a pilgrimage."

When they step inside the restaurant, the pizza faithful may be surprised to find a nebbishy-looking bespectacled man in his fifties with a faded baseball cap.

Born in Brooklyn, Giannone and his wife, Mary Ann, moved to Sheepshead Bay when they got married.

"We met in a bar," he says. "But I recognized her from the train" (on his commute). At one time, they both worked for the Port Authority, in the World Trade Center. Paulie is half Italian, half Jewish—"Kosher Nostra," he jokes—with a longtime passion for pizza. He says he "always loved a good slice and always loved to cook."

Passion was one thing; making a living another. He landed a job as a programmer for AT&T, moving to Lucent and then Avaya before taking a buyout in August 2001. Then he did consulting work in places like Syracuse, New York; Greensboro, North Carolina; and Wilmington, Delaware. "People suggested I open a restaurant. I didn't want to do it. My head was spinning just thinking about it. If I did it, I wanted to do something special, and how could you do something with the greatest chefs in the world around you?"

In the early 1990s, he became a self-described "pizza enthusiast." He had a "pizza epiphany" at Totonno's. He fell in love with the clam pizza at De Lorenzo's Tomato Pies in Trenton, and the Sicilian at L&B Spumoni Gardens. He went on his own pizza tours— Howard Beach, Coney Island, the Village. He started making pizza in a conventional oven at home using flatbread from Corrado's in Jersey, then built a brick oven in his backyard. But he was afraid to go all in.

"My son told me to cut out the crap, stop making excuses." Paulie smiles. "I used to be afraid of commitment; now I embrace it like a friend."

He invited friends to pizza parties at his house and mastered his technique. Confident, he invited bloggers like Kuban and the GoodEater Collaborative's Joshua Levin.

FACT: Independents own 57 percent of pizzerias and constitute 48 percent of sales.

Paulie Gee's is located in an unremarkable stretch of Greenpoint Avenue.

"My whole goal was to get Adam out there," he says of Kuban, founder of the city's most influential pizza blog.

At first, Paulie wanted to open a pizzeria in New Jersey—maybe Madison, maybe Jersey City—but the big city beckoned. A liquor license, which he considered a must, would cost $150,000 in Jersey City; in New York, $505 a year.

"I wrote to the editor of one food site—'Would you write about me if I opened in Jersey City?' The answer was a blunt no. The liquor license pushed me over the edge."

Did he have modest goals? Not quite. "I wanted a Zagat listing; I wanted to be mentioned in the same breath as all these pizzaiolas I admired."

Mathieu Palombino of Motorino and Mark Iacono at Lucali's offered advice.

Williamsburg was too expensive, so Paulie checked out Greenpoint. "All I saw were dollar stores and Polish restaurants. I didn't see any hipsters." He corrects himself. "Don't say 'hipsters.' I was looking for people who locked their bicycles. I didn't have any money for this thing, didn't have a dime, but I was going to do it."

One walk down hip Franklin Street and he was hooked. "There was something special here. I was smitten. There were a lot of bars, and nothing like me."

In the former Paloma restaurant on Greenpoint Avenue, a block from the East River, he found his dream space. The building dates to 1931; it once was a stable and fire station. Paulie signed a lease in November 2009. He started corralling investors—friends, co-workers—and took out a home equity loan. He visited the Manhattan Inn in Greenpoint, was enchanted by its old-timey look—furniture made of recycled materials and such decorative touches as diner sugar shakers turned light fixtures—and hired hOmE, the decorative team responsible for it.

They turned Paulie Gee's into the anti-pizzeria: pumpkin pine floors, wooden booths, creaky doors, a wood-slatted, lamp-dotted catwalk.

On a visit to Nomad Pizza in Hopewell, he became "enamored" with the oven, made by heralded oven builder Stefano Ferrara. Of course he had to buy one. It was shipped from Italy and trucked over to Greenpoint Avenue. Easy part. The wood floor had to be reinforced with beams in the basement ("so the floor wouldn't cave in"), and the three-ton oven had to be put on rollers and squeezed through the door. Tough part. He ended up paying the riggers $5,500. The oven cost $12,000, plus $3,000 for shipping. It was one big headache but "worth every penny," a proud Paulie says.

On March 10, 2011, the night before the restaurant's official opening, Paulie held a party for friends and family. It was a "disaster"—his dough maker "messed up" the dough. Chris Parachini at Roberta's in Bushwick came to the rescue, sending his own dough maker to help Paulie's in his first few days of operation.

By this time, Paulie was a Facebook and Twitter fixture. "Guerrilla marketing," he says with a smile. "I have never spent a dime on advertising."

Despite the buildup, business was just "OK" the first five months. Then he acquired a liquor license, and business doubled.

"You don't make money—you don't make much money—selling pizza," he says wisely. He buys local—his kale is from Eagle Street Rooftop Farm in Greenpoint, his coffee from Oslo Coffee Roasters in Williamsburg. One customer, Mike Kurtz, told Paulie he wanted to learn how to make pizza; Kurtz ended up supplying the hot honey that is now on Paulie Gee's Hellboy pizza. Sea Bean Goods, in Greenpoint, rents his kitchen to make their soups, which are on the menu.

And Paulie Gee? He's in the restaurant every night, schmoozing with customers, making sure everything's all right.

"If a pie's not right, I'll pull it off a customer's table," he says sternly.

There's no delivery, and no slices. His staff dresses in jeans and baseball caps; in the summer, you'll see shorts. Whatever you do, don't walk behind the counter into the kitchen. I followed him once back there and was promptly stopped. "You're not allowed back there," he says. "You never know what you might see."

FACT:
Pizzerias bought about $4 billion in cheese in 2011.

Paulie's basic dough recipe is from Peter Reinhart's *American Pie,* although he constantly experimented with cheese and toppings. The Delboy (fior di latte, Italian tomatoes, Berkshire sopressata picante, and Parmigiano-Reggiano) and the Hellboy (the Delboy with Mike's Hot Honey) are the two most popular pizzas.

His "prohibited Ps"—toppings that will never appear on the menu—are pepperoni, pineapple, poultry, peppers, and potatoes.

The house soundtrack is sixties and seventies rock—2,600 songs in all, with Steve Miller, Procol Harem, the James Gang, Jimi Hendrix blistering through "Hey Joe." Several items are musically minded—among them the Cheek Corea salad (chick peas, pasta, escarole, red onion, olive oil, lemon juice, oven-crisped Berkshire guanciale) and the In Ricotta Da Vita pizza (tomatoes, sweet or vegan sausage, pecorino Romano, baby arugula, ricotta, extra virgin olive oil).

Amid the wooden booths and hippie-era music and bottles of Bengali Tiger IPA, the man with the faded baseball cap and black squarish glasses sits. A look of content if not pleasure is on his face. He has survived his first pizza year.

"It's gone beyond my wildest dreams," he says. "I'm really happy for the first time in my life."

Don't Mess with Ray's or Famous Ray's or . . .

Your first—or last—name is Ray. You want to open a Ray's Pizza in Fort Lauderdale or Kansas City or Albuquerque.

Free piece of advice:

Don't.

"I had a guy in Arizona," says the woman with the jet black hair sitting in the dining room of Ray's Original Famous Pizza on Ninth Avenue. "He had a Ray's Pizza. He said, 'My first name is Ray.' I said, 'I don't care what your name is.' He said, 'I'll have to change the name and all the menus.' I said, 'It's going to cost you a lot more in damages.'"

Agatha Mangano may be the most determined person in New York City. She is the daughter of Rosolino Mangano, who opened Ray's Real Italian Pizza at 59th Street and

Agatha Mangano,
co-owner, Famous Ray's/
Original Famous Ray's.

First Avenue in 1964, the first of what would become an empire of Ray's pizzerias—Ray's. Famous Ray's. Famous Original Ray's. All those names were later trademarked, and Mangano is constantly on the lookout for the most detested word in her vocabulary—"infringers," those who open pizzerias with "Ray's" in the name.

"There was a Ray's on 149th Street in the Bronx," she says. "I called the number. It was disconnected. This was two weeks ago. I'm going to go out there. We just found another in Riverdale. It's Ray's Pizza Express. We're going to send them a cease-and-desist letter. They're going to change the name. I told my attorney, 'I want damages.'"

She says the family spends $50,000 to $75,000 in attorney fees every year protecting the company name. She relies on a network of friends to let her know when another Ray's pops up. When her niece spotted a Ray's Pizza in Ireland on vacation, she called her aunt, who took action.

"I'm determined to get them all," Mangano says. "Stop them. It's what my father built."

Rosolino Mangano emigrated to this country from Sicily. His brother, Angelo, had already been working at a pizzeria on 59th Street and First Avenue.

"The [owners] said to my dad and uncle, why don't you buy the place? So they bought the place."

They renamed it Ray's Real Italian Pizza.

Rosolino Mangano's first store on 59th Street and First Avenue.

Interior, Famous Ray's, Ninth Avenue.

"Nobody knew him as Rosolino; everybody called him Ray," Mangano explains. "It was Ray's Pizza he owned."

In the early 1970s, Rosolino opened Original Ray's Pizza in a former pizzeria at 76th Street and Third Avenue—the first Ray's with "Original Ray's" in its name. In 1973, he opened a Famous Ray's Pizza in a former barbershop at 11th Street and Sixth Avenue. In 1974, he opened another Famous Ray's, at 54th and Seventh Avenue, the oldest of the family's nine current stores.

The first pizzeria to have the name Famous Original Ray's is the one we're sitting in—Ninth Avenue and 23rd Street.

If you think that's confusing, wait until you hear the story of all the other Ray's over the years. Sit down; this can make you dizzy. Most credit Ralph Cuomo with opening the first Ray's, Ray's Pizza, on Spring Street in 1959. Cuomo always said the Italian name for Ralph—Raffaele—was shortened by others to Raffy and then Ray. In the early sixties, Cuomo opened a Ray's on 59th Street; in 1964 it was sold to Mangano, who kept the name.

Agatha Mangano doesn't dispute the Ray's on Prince Street being the first Ray's.

"Ralph was always nice to us," she says. "He said, 'I'm not claiming to be the original Ray.' He said, 'This is the real Ray,' and would point to my dad."

Her dad has said that "Ray" is a shortened version of Rosolino and that he was the one who made the name Ray's famous. In the early 1980s, he sold one of his pizzerias to Gary Esposito, who would go on to open five more Famous Ray's, in New Jersey and Long Island. At one point, he and Cuomo entered into a partnership to franchise Ray's. They applied for a trademark, but Rosolino Mangano intervened, and a legal battle ensued until Mangano joined the partnership in 1990.

Then there's Ray Bari. Actually, there was never a Ray behind Ray Bari; Joseph Bari bought a Ray's Pizza from Rosolino Mangano in 1973,

Rosolino Mangano
at one of his stores.

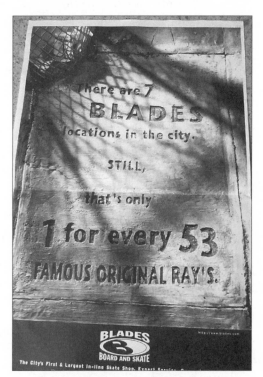

Ad approved by Mangano
family that pokes fun at
all the Rays in the city.

called it Ray Bari's, and later claimed he was the one "who made Ray's popular."

Bari claimed in a 1987 *New York Times* story that he held the rights to the words "Ray's," "Original," and "Famous" as pertaining to pizza. The reporter, William Geist, called Ray's locations around the city asking for Ray. One said it had a "Ray"—the owner, Ralph Cuomo. Check out the story; it's laugh-out-loud funny.

In any event, Cuomo has since passed away, the Ray's on Prince Street closed in October 2011, and the Manganos now hold the rights to "Ray's Pizza" in all its forms.

"All the variations—Ray's Pizza, Original Ray's Pizza, Famous Ray's,

Another Ray's wannabee, this one in Phoenix.

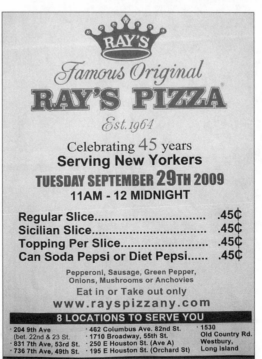

The real Ray's celebrated its forty-fifth anniversary by rolling back the prices.

Famous Original Ray's—are trademarked," Agatha Mangano says. "We're the Ray's of all the Ray's."

The distinctive crown was added to the logo in the 1980s. At Ray's peak, in the 1980s, there were twenty-five stores in the city. There are now eleven.

"Most of the infringers out there have crossed our path," she says. "Most of them were former employees. There are twelve pizzerias called Ray's in Arizona, and they're all trying to copy our crown. They're all cousins and whatever, and they worked for my dad."

Her grandmother in Italy—Maria "Nonna" Mangano—taught her father how to make pizza. Nonna had a brick oven in her house. "She made a Sicilian [pizza]—you'd want to eat the whole thing." Agatha laughs. "We used to go to Italy, come back twenty pounds heavier."

Her mom, Anna, passed away in July 2011. Rosolino Mangano still visits the family stores. "He'll check the sauce, scream at us," his daughter says, laughing.

On Ray's forty-fifth anniversary, in 2009, you could buy plain and Sicilian slices for 45 cents at all the stores. "There were lines around the block. It felt good to give back," Agatha says.

How will the family mark the fiftieth anniversary? "I have a few ideas, but I'm keeping everybody in suspense," Agatha replies.

She doesn't keep any of the infringers in suspense, that's for sure. She hears about them, she goes after them. The first lawsuit was filed in 1989.

Famous Ray's Facebook page offers a slice of history, and a warning:

> We are the Mangano family, the owners of Famous Original Ray's Pizza. The patriarch of our family, Rosolino "Ray" Mangano, started it all. He created the original Ray's Pizza. Today we still follow Ray's recipes.
>
> . . . To be clear, we own federal trademark registrations issued by the United States Patent and Trademark Office for the Ray's Pizza trademarks. Over the years we have systematically taken steps to stop infringers from using our trademarks. We did commence an infringement lawsuit against the operator of the Famous Ray's Pizza located on 11th Street. That lawsuit was recently settled.
>
> We have an important message for all infringers of the Ray's Pizza trademarks: WE WILL STOP YOU. If you want to avoid litigation and the payment of damages STOP NOW.

Her search for "infringers" never ceases. She mentions one non-family-owned Ray's in the city. "I went over there [two years ago]," she says. "I told them, 'This is going to be ugly.' The guy was being nasty, cursed at me. We got a judgment, $89,000 in damages."

The Not Ray's in Brooklyn?

"We've sent him cease-and-desist orders. He ignores the letters."

"St. Marks," she adds, referring to Ray's Pizza Bagel Cafe on St. Marks Place, "is next."

When she confronted the owner of a Ray's in New Jersey, he changed the pizzeria's name to Roy's, but the menu resembled the real Ray's, so Mangano went after them again, and the owner switched to a completely different—and harmless—name.

The family turned down a chance to open thirteen Ray's stands in MetLife Stadium in the Meadowlands, home of the

Menu for a Ray's wannabee.

New York Giants and New York Jets. "It wasn't a good opportunity," she explains. "We weren't going to make any money—they were going to make money."

Agatha's daughter, brother, and several cousins work in the various stores. Her three sisters work in the corporate office, in Brooklyn.

There are no plans to franchise—yet. "Our biggest fear is that we're lose the quality. But maybe we'll franchise in the future."

The Ninth Avenue Ray's has appeared in *Sex and the City* and *Law & Order*. The biggest order ever? Three hundred pizzas for High School for the Humanities on West 18th Street.

"I don't eat nobody else's pizza," Mangano says, almost defiantly. She admits she tried Domino's once ("you're tired of seeing all the commercials"), but never Papa John's or Pizza Hut.

One year, she was on the road for five days in New Jersey, checking on Ray's infringers. She ticks off the towns. "Riverdale. Waldwick. New Brunswick. Piscataway. Montvale. Fairlawn. I took a lot of pictures. We went after all of them."

How did she find out about them? Mangano smiles. "I got friends all over."

The Oldest Italian Cheese Store in the Country

Months of research for this book yielded many great stories, spun masterfully by New Yorkers, masters of the art.

The funniest came from an unlikely source—Alleva Dairy, at the corner of Grand and Mulberry streets in Little Italy.

Those expecting the country's oldest Italian cheese shop to be staid and stuffy and run by rolling-pin-wielding Italian grandmothers will be disappointed. Owner Robert Alleva and his employees good-naturedly taunt each other. And it's hard to imagine one of those Italian grandmas telling the story of the Great Cheese Heist.

Five years ago, several enterprising—not to mention athletic—types broke into the store through the ceiling to steal (you can't make this stuff up) six 110-pound blocks of

Robert Alleva outside his Little Italy cheese shop.

provolone. They somehow lugged the torpedo-shaped cheese up through the ceiling and into a nearby apartment, at which time the caper, like bad cheese, crumbled.

"Within two days this stuff smells," Alleva says. "The neighbors complain, call the police. The provolone's in the apartment. An arrest is made."

The *Post* and *Daily News,* not surprisingly, had fun with the story. Alleva isn't sure, though, how much hard cheese time the burglars served.

Shortly after telling the story, Alleva spots employee George Rogobete, in a winter coat, about to leave the shop to make a delivery.

"George, what are you doing, going to Alaska?" Alleva jokes.

When he returns, Rogobete sniffles. Unfortunately for him, the boss hears it.

"You're always sick," Alleva cracks.

"Always?" says Rogobete, quick with a comeback. "Two times a day is not always."

Alleva's great-grandmother Pina, born in Benevento, Italy, opened the store in 1892 next door to its current location.

"This used to be a bar," Alleva explains. "During Prohibition, the bar closed up, the cheese moved over here."

His great-grandmother may have started the business, but his grandfather Henry made a "science" out of cheese making.

FACT:
The country's highest-grossing single-unit independent pizzeria is the Moose's Tooth Pub and Pizzeria in Anchorage.

38

George Rogobete, who works at Alleva Dairy.

"Our calling card was always mozzarella and ricotta," says Alleva. "It was always cheese, never meats."

Today, you can get a nice Italian sandwich at Alleva, but cold cuts didn't make an appearance in the store until 1980 or so. Alleva started working in the store when he was eleven. He would later earn a degree in medical technology but admits he was "never cut out for the nine-to-five briefcase crowd." "I'd see these guys at the train station in their little uniforms," he says sarcastically.

Today, Alleva makes three thousand to four thousand pounds of mozzarella a week; 70 percent of the store's business is from September to December. The nation's oldest cheese shop supplies the nation's oldest pizzeria—Lombardi's, four blocks away. "That relationship has been forever," according to Alleva.

Neon sign outside Alleva Dairy.

So, how does one know mozzarella is fresh?

"You can't go by color," Alleva replies. "The mozzarella can turn yellow in the water. It should be smooth. If it's been sitting in the water too long, it gets a little stringy and rough. And it should taste like milk. When you eat it, there should be liquid coming out."

Cheese making may not be rocket science, but you need to pay attention.

"What you're doing is mixing the raw curd with milk and water. The butterfat holds it all together. Without the butterfat you don't have flavor and consistency. You have to know when to take [the mozzarella balls] out. When it's ready, you got to get it out, you've got to rock and roll."

Alleva admits he doesn't offer a "huge" selection of cheeses. There is the homemade mozzarella and ricotta, plus imported Parmesan, provolone, Romano, aged pecorino, fontina, asiago, taleggio, Swiss Gruyère, Danish blue, Sicilian pepper cheese, and several others.

"I don't get into the truffle cheeses," Alleva says dismissively. "Or cheeses with pistachio inside, things like that."

The most popular imported cheese is Parmigiano-Reggiano, but his favorite is fontina ("soft and creamy, not too salty").

The store—tile floors, tin ceiling—also serves as an old-time Italian grocery, with shelves stocked with Quadratini bite-sized wafer cookies, Balconi Mix Max sponge cakes, Colussi crackers, Bertagni spinach-and-ricotta ravioli, La Montanara figs with almonds, Napoletani pasta, Battistero panettone, Sicilian anchovies, capers with Sicilian sea salt, cans of scungilli, and jars of solid tuna. There are several dozen kinds of balsamic and red wine vinegars, dozens more bottles of extra-virgin olive oil. Sausage and sopressata are draped over a steel bar.

The shop also makes its own rice and ricotta balls, bruschetta, and broccoli rabe; during the week, there's homemade eggplant parm, lasagna, meatballs, chicken parm.

Plaque for long-gone store outside Alleva Dairy.

"For the city, we have a lot of space," Alleva says of his 1,600-square-foot store. "City people usually work out of shoeboxes."

He's proud the store has stayed open a hundred-plus years, but how much longer he doesn't know. His great-grandmother worked into her nineties—she would ride the bus in from Brooklyn every day. The current owner is just fifty-eight but says he may be the last Alleva in the business.

"I think I may the last man standing," Alleva explains. "My son has a good job [elsewhere]. It's a seven-day business. You try to take a day off here and there, but people expect you to be here. I want to be here; there are certain things I have to watch. I'm never off for more than a week. As soon as I leave, the refrigerator or something else breaks.

"I think I'll just lock it up," he adds. "I'm not going to sell it with my name out there. But we'll see. We have a few years."

Joe's on Carmine

Joe Pozzuoli, standing outside his Greenwich Village pizzeria, excuses himself for a minute. It's time to make a pizza delivery in his car.

Pozzuoli—low throaty voice, gold chain around his neck—is seventy-five years old.

The founder of Joe's on Carmine Street, a classic New York City slice joint, may not make many pizzas anymore, but he's always around Joe's, which friends told him wouldn't last a year.

Joe's Pizza opened in 1975 (Saigon falls, Watergate principals sentenced, *Jaws* premieres), and neither the old-school pizzeria nor the old man seems in any danger of slowing down.

"I never take day off," he says in his distinct Italian accent. "One Christmas many years ago I tried, but it didn't work out. People complained—'you weren't here.' So I never did it again."

Born in 1937, he came to this country in 1956. "From Naples—Capua, Caserta," he says, naming his town and province. Pozzuoli is also a city near Naples. Its most famous native son or daughter: Sophia Loren, born in a hospital charity ward.

"You better cut the pizza in four pieces because I'm not hungry enough to eat six."
—Yogi Berra

Joe Pozzuoli, owner of Joe's on Carmine.

In 1959, Pozzuoli opened a pizzeria in Boston called Pino's. Several more stores followed, including one in Kenmore Square, near Fenway Park.

"We used to make pizza in the window. People would walk by, they'd clap their hands. It was 35 cents a slice. No, 15 cents a slice."

Michael Valerio, founder of Papa Gino's, once worked at Pozzuoli's Washington Street store in Boston. In 1961, Valerio opened his first pizzeria, Piece of Pizza, just down the street; in 1968, it became Papa Gino's.

In the meantime, Pozzuoli moved back to Italy—"my mother didn't want to live in America anymore," his son, Joe, says, smiling—but returned in 1975, settling in Bay Ridge. But Pozzuoli

Delivering Joe's Pizza to that desert island.

42

Customers check out the wall at Joe's.

dreamed of opening a pizzeria in Greenwich Village, and he craved the prime corner of Carmine and Bleecker.

"I liked the location. But I was going in green. People told me I would never last."

He lasted, all right. In 2005, his lease was up, and he couldn't afford the rent increase, so Pozzuoli scrambled for another location. He got lucky—a vacant storefront three doors down. It once housed Golden Pizza; it turned into a gold mine for Pozzuoli. A competitor moved into his original location; he didn't last a year.

Joe Pozzuoli with popular sixties wrestler Haystacks Calhoun.

Joe's offers a classic New York slice, thinner and crispier than most. The interior is spare—exactly one table, in the center of the room—but inviting, with green tile and white walls. The prime dining spot: a ledge by the sidewalk window, open in warmer weather.

The first celebrity customer at Joe's, according to its founder, was Jane Fonda. Leonardo DiCaprio, Matthew Broderick, Michelle Rodriguez, and Kiefer Sutherland have all eaten at Joe's. The

Conan O'Brien
served as guest pizza
maker for a TV spot.

pizzeria appeared in a scene in *Superman II.* On this particular day, a twenty-something actor strides purposefully from the sidewalk to the front door again and again rehearsing a scene for—even Joe doesn't know what for.

"They just show up," he says with a shrug of his shoulders.

Same with his customers, at all hours. Joe's opens at 10 A.M., stays open until 5 A.M. It's open Thanksgiving, Christmas, and New Year's. "The busiest day of the year is New Year's Eve," Pozzuoli explains. "It is crazy. People coming in from the clubs."

He eats at least one slice a day; in fact, breakfast often consists of a cup of coffee and a slice. Alex, his main pizza maker, has been here twenty-five years. Joe still makes pizza when needed.

"Busy nights, I'm there. Crazy nights. Oh, yeah."

In a typical week, Joe's makes about 1,500 pizzas. You'll never wait long for a fresh slice; the 600-degree oven cooks pizzas in five minutes, and customer traffic is constant. You can get a whole pizza, but the quintessential Joe's experience is a fresh hot slice. There are no calzones or garlic knots or any of that other nonsense.

The mozzarella is from an Italian deli in Brooklyn; the regular cheese is Grande; the sauce is made from crushed San Marzano tomatoes.

"No pizza sauce here," Pozzuoli says, as if that were an indictable offense.

"This is the same slice you got in 1975," his son points out.

"That's very rare. Everybody goes through trends."

"It's the same pizza since '58, '59," his father corrects him.

Time for Joe to go; he has a doctor's appointment.

"I'm seventy-five," he says, "and still on top of it."

When will he retire?

"Retire to what?" he says, almost offended. "What am I gonna do?"

Pizza box,
Joe's on Carmine.

Miki

It takes maybe five minutes to convince you that Miki Agrawal multitasks like nobody's business.

She talks to me for several minutes at a window table, leaves to greet a friend; returns and talks a few more minutes; pauses to text someone; asks her manager, David Haynes, a question; talks some more; gets up to chat with a friend in the corner; takes a phone call; asks one of her pizza makers a question; returns to pick up our conversation exactly where we left off; is up again several minutes later to greet someone else . . .

Did I mention that prior to all this she conducted a pizza-making class with a roomful of loud, fidgety teenage kids?

"Do you want me to give you a massage, Dave?" she kids Haynes, who's complaining of various aches and pains.

"No," he says, smiling, "I'll just go to Chinatown."

Agrawal is one of the few women in an overwhelmingly male-dominated business. She's in her early thirties but could pass for a student at Cornell University, which she attended. SLICE, which she opened in the fall of 2005 with her twin sister, Radha, is not simply yet another hip pizzeria in a city threatening to be overrun with them. SLICE uses fresh, seasonal, local ingredients; the pizzas feature whole wheat and herb crusts, organic low-fat mozzarella, and atypical toppings like chicken sausage, sautéed wild mushrooms, chicken tikka masala, and truffled ricotta. The menu is free of pretension; a marinara and

Miki Agrawal,
owner of SLICE.

mozzarella pizza is called the Simpleton. Can't make up your mind? You can order a "flight" of four pizzas, like a beer sampler at a brew pub. Slices run $5 to $7, which may make them the city's priciest.

Born in Canada, Miki was raised in a highly competitive family ("we had to get a 4.0 GPA"). She and her sister attended school seven days a week in Montreal: French school Monday through Friday; Japanese school on Saturday; Hindi school on Sunday. In high school, she kept the high grades—and played soccer, field hockey, and badminton.

Miki and her
twin sister, Radha.

Her oldest sister attended Harvard ("the oldest sister is always the smartest'); Miki and Radha headed to Cornell.

"My parents said we could leave Canada if we went to an Ivy League school," she says. Miki majored in business and communication, studied a year in London, and after graduation searched for an investment banking job in New York.

In 2001, she was working for Deutsche Bank. That summer, she had moved into a new apartment in Brooklyn Heights. Her commute

Message board on
sidewalk outside SLICE.

took her by subway under the World Trade
Center every morning. On September 10, she
was out late with friends; the next morning she
slept through her alarm clock.

She left Deutsche Bank that year to play
professional soccer with the New York Magic.

Then came work as a production assistant
on film shoots. "I chauffeured people around,
got coffee." She laughs. "Here I am, with this
Cornell education."

She worked her way up to production
manager. Then she developed a stomach ailment
and discovered she, along with about 80 percent
of the world, was lactose-intolerant. That led to
research on organic and vegan cheeses.

"I thought, 'Pizza is a $32 billion industry and no one is making it better for you.'"

Agrawal, a self-described "very impatient person," assembled her "smartest" friends,
informed them she needed to raise "a couple hundred thousand dollars," did so, and
opened SLICE on the Upper East Side.

"I had no idea what I was doing," she confesses. Her staff was no better—"all these
amateurs messing up."

David Haynes,
manager of SLICE.

A storefront opened up on
Hudson Street, in the West Village.
"Screw it, let's do it," she told herself
and opened a second SLICE.

She fired everyone who had
worked for her on the Upper East
Side (her approach, then and now, is
"hire slowly, fire quickly") and started
with a new staff and outlook.

"Team matters," she explains.
"Everyone has to get along, from the
dishwasher to the general manager.
How they mesh together creates that
magic."

Sign inside SLICE.

She found Haynes on Craigslist and hired a new chef, Jose Martinez, a former pastry chef for Todd English's Plaza Food Hall.

"If he goes off to another big-name [restaurant], he won't have as much fun," she says, smiling. "And he won't be treated as well."

SLICE is located in the West Village, which she calls "the most sought-after neighborhood in New York," and expenses can be astronomical. Her rent is nearly $7,500 a month, plus utilities. She pays the city a $10,000 annual fee for tables on the sidewalk.

In the move from East Side to West Village, the menu received a face-lift; there are now soups, salads, vegetable antipasto, seasonal pastas, and desserts like Brazilian bread pudding and SLICE Cream-Wich, a chocolate chip cookie with cinnamon-infused crème Chantilly. The beers and wines are locally sourced—Brooklyn Brewery, Sixpoint, Shmaltz Brewing, Onabay Vineyards, and others.

Momentarily at rest at the corner table, Agrawal orders a flight of pizzas from her own kitchen and is curious to know her guest's opinion. "That combination of sweet, salty, tangy—how does it all work in your mouth?" she asks.

She regards pizza as "the absolutely perfect combination of carbs and protein. It fulfills all the major food groups. It's a perfect balance. It's front lobe food, the food that you crave."

Miki drops off free pizzas to companies in the hopes they'll hire SLICE for catering events. She hopes to open a SLICE in Brooklyn. She and John Arena, owner of Metro Pizza in Las Vegas, opened SLICE Las Vegas in April 2012. She and Arena are working on a book titled *Give Pizza Chance*, about "the history of civilization through the eyes of a pizza adult."

"I thought I'd have ten stores by now," she says. "So I'll have three. My definition of success has changed a lot in six years. First it was, how much money can I make? Now I'm appreciating the process. There's a great saying—it takes ten years to be an overnight success."

The Magic Pizza Bus

The twenty-five pizza acolytes—from Queens to Calgary—sit raptly at Luzzo's in the East Village, eyes on the man they will follow anywhere, as long as it involves pizza.

"A wood flame flickers, a coal flame smolders," Scott Wiener begins.

"This oven is the same temperature as Lombardi's, but it cooks a lot faster. That wood inside the oven, that flicker of flame in a live fire? That's going to inspire activity out of the yeast . . . you end up getting a softer crust. The higher the temperature, the faster the bake, the softer the crust."

Several of his "students" take notes in the tiny spiral-bound notebooks Wiener passed out at Lombardi's, the first stop on what you could call Dough 101.

Others are probably wondering when they'll need to unwrap one of the lemon suckers, included in the official Pizza Tour Survival Kit, to counterattack all the cheese they'll be eating today.

Scott Wiener, owner,
Scott's Pizza Tours.

You never know when you're going to need some pizza flour.

Wiener applies some spice to a pizza.

Others, like Rachel Shoichet, a kindergarten teacher in Brooklyn, are more relaxed; this is the third time she's taken one of Wiener's pizza bus tours. That's nothing; a couple from Denver has taken the tour twelve times.

Pizza—the product and topic—can get old, but the energetic, excitable Wiener, who once played in bands called Bikini Car Wash and Martha Dumptruck Massacre, always makes it sound new and fresh.

"Some people deliver pizza to the people," he says. "I deliver the people to the pizza."

There are several pizza-themed walking or bus tours in the city, but none of their leaders have the background or knowledge Wiener does. He's visited flour mills, bufala mozzarella farms, cannery operations, and a pizza box manufacturer in Italy; eaten at legendary Naples pizzerias; done consulting work for restaurants; led private tours for the likes of Google, Yahoo, and Pizza Hut; and led walking tours in snowstorms.

"Most of the time people are hard core," he says in the yellow school bus he rents for his trips. "Look at this posse. Hard core."

Scott's Pizza Tours does a walking tour every day except Tuesday and Sunday, while the bus tours are Sunday only. The bus tours usually start at Lombardi's—this is the country's first pizzeria, after all—and take in three other stops. It is a mark of Wiener's influence that he is allowed to bring his group into Lombardi's before it opens and take them into the kitchen.

He lugs a pizza delivery box full of T-shirts and entertains bus passengers with his "pizza mega-mix" ("Jive Talking," "Won't Get Fooled Again," plus a pizza song in which German schoolchildren bravely try to speak English, and other loony tunes).

At Luzzo's, he tells the group, basil is put on pizza before it's placed in the oven; at Lombardi's, basil is added after the pizza is done.

"It's a huge debate in the pizza world, when to put on the basil," he explains. "I'd put it on after. The point of the whole basil is not the leaf but the oils in the leaf. If the oils don't get out to the rest of the pizza, there's no flavor."

You're not going to find this stuff readily on the Internet, and there is something about Wiener's infectious enthusiasm that draws his "pizza buddies" back time and again.

How did the guy with the perfect hot dog name get so caught up in pizza? He grew up in the Jersey burbs. Every Wednesday night was pizza night in the Wiener household.

"I got into pizza deeper when I went to college [Syracuse] and got introduced to crappy pizza," he says. "Rubber cheese, spongy dough, dollar slices you eat late at night. It was warm and it was cheap."

Only when he toured cross-country with his band between semesters did he start to notice regional differences in pizza.

In 2003, Wiener visits Sally's Apizza in New Haven and a world begins to reveal itself. He starts reading *Slice*, the pizza blog. His brother finds a copy of *Pizza Today* in an Italian restaurant and gives Wiener the subscription card. He makes connections. Jeremy White, editor of *Pizza Today*, invites him to pizza conventions.

Wiener works for a while as a sound engineer for the city of Hoboken ("I would grab a slice, put up a flyer, grab a slice, put up a flyer"). Then friends start asking him to take them to all these great pizzerias he kept talking about—Totonno's, Di Fara, and others. For his birthday in 2007, he hires a bus and takes twenty-eight friends on a whirlwind pizza tour—Famous Original Ray's, Patsy's, Fanny's, six in all. It is not quite the polished effort the bus tours are today.

Wiener attacks a giant slice at Benny Tudino's in Hoboken while on the Star-Ledger's Pizza Patrol.

"We ordered by phone, ate pizza on the bus," he recalls. "I didn't know much about the styles of pizza. It was more like, eat pizza, have a conversation about it."

One of the bus passengers, though, is Adam Kuban, founder of *Slice*, who posts an online item about the tour titled "The Pizza Express." The e-mails and phone calls start pouring in. Time to get serious. Wiener enrolls in free city classes in marketing and bookkeeping and takes the 150-question licensed tour guide test. Which he promptly flunks. "I studied my ass off and passed it the next time."

In February 2008, he meets with Lombardi's and pitches the idea of starting his pizza tour there. To his surprise ("I had this scraggly beard at the time, and was living on a boat"), they agree.

The *Daily News* sends a photographer to his first official tour. "I had no idea what I was doing; I was really nervous. Luckily it went off without a hitch," he recalls. The subsequent full-page story earns him serious exposure.

Since the first formal tour in April 2008, Wiener has taken his charges to thirty different pizzerias. He always calls the scheduled pizzeria the day before to make sure space is available and to check that their oven is not "funky." You know, having a bad day for whatever reason.

As they sit down at Lombardi's this particular day, tour-goers are handed their official Pizza Tour Survival Kit—spiral-bound notebook, lemon suckers, tutte frutti gummi pizzas "palate cleansers," and a moist towelette.

"This company sent me ten thousand packets," he says of the towelettes. "I'm using you guys to get rid of them."

"This is the first licensed pizzeria in the United States," he says at Lombardi's. "Almost all of the seventy-six thousand pizzerias that are part of the [$35 billion] pizza business started as a business like this. You have all the competing stories—pizza began in Greece, pizza began in China. Today we're talking about pizza—a dough that's stretched and baked."

After Lombardi's, they board the waiting yellow school bus for the short ride to Luzzo's. "See the red building on the corner?" Wiener says as the bus stops on Bowery. "That's the only pizza oven factory in the city."

At Luzzo's, he spots the bottles of Super Tuscan Extra Virgin Olive Oil on each table and says, "This is legit good oil."

The sauces at both Lombardi's and Luzzo's are not cooked, just spread on the pizzas before they're placed in the oven. Luzzo's adds olive oil to its sauce, Lombardi's does not. It's insider pizza knowledge, and Wiener's students are loving it.

"You gotta remember," he says on the bus, "Rome didn't have pizza until after New York. Pizza comes from Naples."

The third stop is J&V Pizzeria in Bensonhurst, a classic slice joint. Wiener calls the crust "potent, robust," and takes note of the "super-clear translucent onions." There is mention of "cheese drag," "the poke test," and "pre-docked" pizzas.

FACT:
Willis HRH offers pizza delivery insurance.

Late afternoon, Totonno's, Coney Island.

Kitschy interior, Pugsley's Pizza, the Bronx.

Famous Original Ray's, Ninth Avenue, Manhattan.

Pizza mural, Famous Original Ray's, Ninth Avenue, Manhattan.

Neon, Ray's Pizza Bagel Cafe, Manhattan.

Scott Wiener
at the end of one of
his school bus tours.

Shannon Hendry,
John's on Bleecker,
Manhattan.

John Solis, a first-timer
at Di Fara, Brooklyn.

Still life, Di Fara, Brooklyn.

Sausage pizza, Denino's,
Staten Island.

Mural outside Roberta's, Bushwick.

Slices, Valducci's pizza truck, Manhattan.

Nickola and Carsten Nordsieck commemorate their heart-shaped pizza at Pizza a Casa.

Mural by Dima (Dmitri Drjuchin) outside L'asso, Manhattan.

Susan Bagali, John's of Elmhurst, Queens.

Ready to be eaten, John's of Elmhurst, Queens.

A kiss is not just a kiss when it's in front of 99¢ Fresh Pizza, Ninth Avenue, Manhattan.

Ronny Barca, owner of
Catania's Pizzeria & Cafe,
the Bronx.

The great Louie & Ernie's, the Bronx.

Sidewalk sign, Majestic Pizza, the Bronx.

Colorful mural, Paesano's Pizza & Pasta, the Bronx.

Another late-night subway stop on my pizza journey.

Neon sign, Brooklyn.

Mural, Bergen Pizza, Brooklyn.

Best Pizza, Williamsburg.

Henry's Pizzeria,
Bushwick.

Pizza Tour participants get ready to chow down inside Sam's Restaurant in Brooklyn.

The last stop is Sam's Restaurant & Pizzeria on Court Street in Brooklyn, where the group meets Lou Migliaccio, Sam's ebullient owner.

Shoichet, the kindergarten teacher in Brooklyn, can't get enough of pizza, or the tour; she'll be back for another one.

"Pizza is the perfect food," she says. "It's got your vegetables, your carbohydrates, your protein."

Wiener has been asked to launch a pizza tour in Rome. Besides the regular walking and bus tours, he stays busy giving private tours—from small groups to "crazy big companies."

"Birthdays, bachelorette parties," he adds. "Just women drinking and listening to me talk for four hours. Crazy."

He figures he eats pizza 320 or 330 days a year.

"Sometimes you eat a slice without realizing you ate a slice," he explains. "I eat pizza constantly. I have to make an effort not to eat it. When I eat pizza, it just happens." He makes pizza at home; on his iPhone are photos of every pizza he's made—two hundred in all—in the past year and a half. In his room are nearly 180 pizza boxes from thirty countries.

"My goal is to have [a box for] every country that has pizza. I've got Lichtenstein, China. I'm going to Belgium for my brother's wedding. I'll be psyched to get a box from Belgium. I've got Australia."

He devours *Pizza Today, PMQ Pizza Magazine*, even *Canadian Pizza Magazine* for news and tips. He reads books on cheese, bread making, tomato growing; in his bag today is a book titled *Extra Virginity: The Sublime and Scandalous World of Olive Oil.*

The pizza man's education is never-ending.

The tours, he maintains, are "not a profit center. I have to live in an apartment with other guys. My goal is not to build this into a large company. I'm not going to have a bus that's wrapped as long as I can exist."

In late afternoon, the tour over, the yellow school bus pulls over on Bowery. The curly-haired guy with the pizza delivery bag slung over his shoulder has some final words of wisdom.

"Continue to enjoy pizza the rest of your life," he tells the group. "Enjoy a slice tonight."

John's on Bleecker

The guy with the piercing blue eyes, tattoos on both arms, and pencil-thin goatee leans back in his office, where bills, time sheets, drawings from schoolkids, his own art, fax machines, chin-up bars, and a bowl full of rubber bands struggle for space.

"Some of the history of this place is hazy," Michael Frank says. "A lot of the guys are dead."

This much is known about John's Pizzeria on Bleecker Street. John Sasso—like Antonio Pero from Totonno's, a former employee at Lombardi's—opened John's in 1929. The pizzas are made in 800-degree coal-fired brick ovens. No credit cards, no reservations, and most important, no slices.

According to its website, John's remains in its original location, but its general manager is not so sure.

"That's up for debate," Frank says. "He [Sasso] may have started in an apartment on MacDougal Street. There was a phone number and address [for John's Pizza] on MacDougal."

Michael Frank, manager of John's on Bleecker.

Neon sign, John's on Bleecker.

Sasso passed away in the late 1970s; his nephew Augustine Vesche, known as Chubby, took over.

"They would sit around in their white T-shirts, smoking, with a glass of wine, make pizza," Frank recalled.

How did a Jersey guy—Frank grew up in Sayreville—end up running John's? Chubby was an uncle to Frank's stepfather, who owns 60 percent of John's.

"He kind of dumped [the business] into my lap," Frank says of his stepfather. "When I was thirteen, he would bring me in, let me bus tables, clean up in the basement. He would throw me a few bucks."

Frank's first real job was as dishwasher at the late great Club Bene in Sayreville, where he would catch the Ramones, Johnny Winter, and other acts. His "hippie uncle" lived in his parents' basement for a time; when he moved out, Frank inherited his vinyl record collection.

Frank graduated from high school and worked in recording studios, playing in a band on the side. He took over as manager of John's in 1992, but he's still a musician,

You can carve your initials or a message on the walls at John's.

Note from soldier stationed in South Korea, "8,435 miles from John's," saying it had been 305 days since he last had a John's pizza.

playing in two bands—Four Year Beard and Stink Stank Stunk. He also started a record label, 7th & Bleecker Arts Entertainment.

Frank calls himself John's general manager, then reconsiders.

"This place runs itself. I'm here to pay the bills, make sure there's no bull—. I don't know how to describe myself. Maybe a babysitter."

Customers have carved their names and initials on the walls; feel free to add your own. The front dining room, with its formidable wooden booths, has been around from the beginning; the side dining room was added in the 1980s. It once housed Matt Umanov's vintage guitar shop; when Umanov moved across the street, John's acquired the space.

Sometimes distributors will run out of sauce or cheese and Frank will be forced to switch to another product temporarily. John's regulars will notice the difference and let Frank know, to his bemusement.

"You gotta roll with it," he says. "It's life."

The menu lists fifty-four pizzas and reads like a *Monty Python* skit—cheese, tomato sauce, onion; cheese, tomato sauce, pepperoni; cheese, tomato sauce, sausage; and so on. Frank didn't see a need to list every imaginable combination, so he shortened the menu. The outrage was immediate.

"The new menu didn't last long—about a week,"

Pizza makers,
John's on Bleecker.

he says. "It was, 'I've been coming here for years, I always had the thirty-two [cheese, sauce, sausage, meatballs, mushrooms].'" Frank laughs. "They made me put [the old menu] back."

Asked to describe the pizza, Frank shrugs his shoulders. "I would just call it, s——, I don't know, it defines the essence of old-school New York pizza."

And that means a coal-fired brick oven, never gas or electric.

"That would change everything. The flavor would not be the same. Coal enables you to get such a high temperature. It cooks faster, it crisps faster, what it does to the molecules in the dough [can't be duplicated]."

Customers? Locals, tourists—especially from France and Japan—and some famous faces.

"Jack Black comes in, he'll eat a whole damn pie by himself. Plain. Doesn't want to put anything on it because it would ruin it. Bruce Springsteen and Jon Stewart were in together recently. Before Johnny Depp moved to France, he would come in. Really cool guy. He liked to talk to the workers. Always hungry for knowledge."

John's "babysitter" is sometimes pressed into service to make pizzas, and he doesn't like it at all.

"It's hard. When you're not used to standing in front of an 800-degree oven, it's hot, it's tough."

On a street filled with pizza—Keste, Pizza Box, Pizza Roma, Bleecker Street Pizza, among others—John's holds its own.

"Friday night, it's packed," the guy with the tattooed arms says. "Saturday rocks. Sunday is insane. That's our busiest day."

Best time to visit: weekdays between 3 and 7 P.M.

Frank eats pizza every other week or so and is not ashamed to admit he sometimes goes the frozen route.

Anjeza Cereni, waitress at John's on Bleecker.

"I recommend Freschetta highly," he says. "Delicious. And cold pizza is the best hangover medicine. Right out of the fridge. The sauce gets you back on point. The sauce soaks up the bile. I definitely recommend cold pizza as a hangover cure."

Best Move I Ever Make

It's 12:15 on a cold, rainy Wednesday afternoon, and a dozen anxious customers are patiently standing outside the storefront on Avenue J.

Domenico DeMarco, owner of the Brooklyn pizzeria that appears at the top of many best-pizza-in-New-York lists, sits at a table in his austere, green-walled dining room, telling a reporter his story. If he is worried about opening late, he does not show it.

Domenico DeMarco, owner
of Di Fara Pizza, Brooklyn.

"My parents were farmers," says DeMarco, born in Provincia di Caserta, outside Naples. "Olive oil, bread, corn, tomatoes, figs. Nineteen fifty-nine, I come to this country. I am twenty-two, twenty-three years old."

Today, the family farm is run by his brothers, John and Angelo.

"I am supposed to be there," DeMarco says, smiling mischievously, "but I am here."

Exterior, Di Fara's.

Of all the city's most heralded pizzerias, Di Fara's is the most humble in appearance. There are two old card tables, the kind you'd normally see in someone's basement, and thirteen chairs. An ancient wooden cash register, tile floors, fluorescent lighting, three ceiling fans. Forks and spoons in a smudged three-drawer cabinet near the window. A map of Campania, and worn prints of Vesuvius and the Leaning Tower of Pisa. An unremarkable brown-lettered marquee.

59

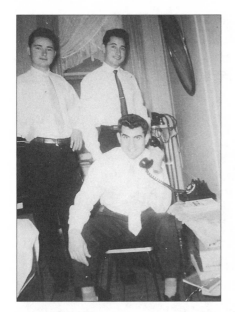

Domenico DeMarco
with his brothers.

Every morning, DeMarco's daughter, Margaret, rolls up the iron gate at the front. She and her sister, Louisa, take orders, answer the phone, order supplies. Three of their five brothers—Michael, Alex, and Dominick Jr.—also work at the pizzeria. But only one person ever makes the pizza—Dad.

"When I come to the United States, I had nobody," DeMarco explains. "My father's friend sent me to a farm in Huntington [Long Island]."

"How many years did you work there?"

A hearty laugh. "Three months."

He and his brother would later open a pizzeria on 59th Street in Sunset Park.

"I wasn't happy there," he says. "Lot of problems. Break-ins. Someone pointed a gun at me." He shrugs. "I didn't call the cops."

One Saturday night, he was walking down Avenue J and couldn't help but notice what was going on.

"The street was crowded, so many people. I saw a For Rent sign. I take the store." Smile. "Best move I ever make."

A similar statement is the title of Margaret Emily MacKenzie's excellent seventeen-minute documentary on Di Fara's—*The Best Thing I Ever Done* (available on Vimeo).

Margaret Mieles,
daughter of
Domenico DeMarco.

Wooden cash register, menu board at Di Fara's.

DeMarco and partner Frank Farina named the pizzeria Di Fara—a contraction of DeMarco and Farina. Today, the storefront on Avenue J, steps from the B and Q subway stop, is the scene of daily theater involving a slightly stooped, grandfatherly man behind the counter. Patience is key to the pizza experience here. Margaret studiously writes down each order on a yellow legal pad ("It uses the brain more, exercises the mind," she explains). Each pizza is made painstakingly, one by one. If you ordered a whole pizza, take a seat and wait for your name to be called. It may take a while.

There is a Regular Pie and a Square Pie, and slices have been $5 since July 2009. At the time, the $1 price increase brought the predictable lamentations from press and general public that this was surely the end of the world.

And yet the lines kept forming outside Di Fara's, rain, cold, snow, whatever.

"It made us more . . . interesting," says Margaret, searching for the right word. "There was the rare occasion when I'd get a hate letter."

A slice of Sicilian, Di Fara's.

Ordering a whole pie seems the best route for those with pizza sticker shock. A whole Regular is $28; a Square, $32.

Zagat's, which rated Di Fara the city's best pizza for eight straight years, has labeled DeMarco a "rock star." Some reports have described the pizza man as moody, domineering; he was kind and helpful on my visit. The pizzeria's own website refers to the "infamous" Di Fara, without explaining why it earns that tag.

Free postcards titled "Di Fara's Freehand Recipe" lay on the mythology a little thick:

Popping crackling Golden Bertolli! kisses the fresh dough.
Tomatoes from Salerno
Buffalo mozzarella from Caserta,
and Fior di Latte,
and Parmigiano Reggiano
Mysterious burnt bubbles
hissing virgin olive oil
slow & steady
spreading dough for the Grand Experiment.

The family opened a Las Vegas store—Dom DeMarco's Pizzeria & Bar—in late 2011 and is hoping to open a Di Fara's in Red Bank, New Jersey.

Patiently waiting for pizza, Di Fara's.

DeMarco is forthright about his pizza making, unlike other high-end pizzeria owners who shroud their work in Vatican-worthy secrecy.

"Every day I experiment," he says. "I start with fresh mozzarella. Italian tomatoes. Grana Padana. Parmigiano-Reggiano. The secret of the pizza is the oven. I keep it very hot. Nine hundred degrees. The pizza stays in too long, it gets dry."

His tomatoes, not surprisingly, are San Marzano.

"They're the best. They're only grown in one place, near Salerno. The ground is very dry. In the north, the land is very rich. No good. You need dry ground."

"You can get good tomatoes in California . . ."

"No comparison," he says, shaking his head.

He uses La Regina di San Marzano plum tomatoes, pulling one out of the jar and handing it over to his visitor for sampling.

The boss shows up at 9 A.M. to make the dough. From 4 to 6 P.M. Di Fara closes; call it the pizza siesta.

"That's what they do in Italy," DeMarco explains. "I sit down, have a glass of wine."

At 9 P.M. sharp, Di Fara's closes.

You can call the pizzeria to order a pizza, but not for that day.

"They can't leave an order on voice mail because that would be insane," Margaret says. "Unless it's for the future."

"If you leave a message and say I'll be there in an hour . . ."

She smiles. "Not happening."

For many years, the pizzeria on Avenue J was relatively unknown. The breakthrough came in 1998, when Jim Leff, founder of *Chowhound*, mentioned Di Fara in his book, *The Eclectic Gourmet Guide to Greater New York City*.

In 2001, the *New York Times*'s Eric Asimov "unleashes the hordes," according to Adam Kuban on *Slice*, when he wrote about Di Fara in the "$25 and Under" column. Packs of pizza lovers descended on Avenue J.

"TV crews from Japan and China have been here," DeMarco says. "Amazing. I cannot believe."

In a back room where the dough is made, he takes a sip of Stappj Gassosa, a lemon-flavored mineral water. There is a block of Grande mozzarella on a table.

"They [a supplier] sent us this; we don't approve," Margaret says.

They'll use it, but today only. Her father normally uses Polly-O whole milk mozzarella, which he mixes with the Parmigiano-Reggiano.

In the dining room, regulars and first-timers wait for their pizzas.

Al Berger, longtime patron of Di Fara's.

"Forty-seven years ago, opening day, I was here," says Al Berger, who grew up several blocks away and now lives in Sheepshead Bay. "He gave away pizza for two hours."

John Solis, an electrician, is here for the first time. "If someone says 'this is the best,' I'll go out and try it," says the Queens resident, whose favorite pizzeria is La Villa in Howard Beach.

It is Lily Fraza's first visit. Her favorite New York pizzerias: Lucali's, Totonno's, and Caruso's, all in Brooklyn.

"Outstanding," she says of the Di Fara slice. "I'm enjoying the crust. All the ingredients seem to be premium."

By 1 P.M., all the chairs are occupied; a nurse eats her slice while leaning against a wall. In a corner, Berger, who as a kid would stop in at Di Fara after stickball games, takes it all in and smiles.

"This guy is like an artist," he says of DeMarco. "He's in a zone when he makes pizza. He doesn't talk to you; you're not there. People leave here, they bless him; he's like Michelangelo."

Denino's

Pizza. Staten Island. Denino's. The three go together like "traffic jams" and "Outerbridge Crossing."

There are other first-rate pizzerias in the forgotten borough—Joe and Pat's and Lee's Tavern, among others—but to understand this pizza island, you start at the corner of Port Richmond and Hooker, and the woman sitting at a table in the back dining room.

Palma Denino, co-owner of Denino's, Staten Island.

64

"Most of the land around here once belonged to a Mrs. Forge," Palma Denino is saying.

"Who was she?"

"A very rich woman," says Palma, not missing a beat.

Carlo Denino, her husband, started serving pizza at Denino's Tavern in 1951, after he came out of the navy. His father, Giovanni, had arrived in America in 1887 from Sicily, opening a confectionary in Staten Island's Port Richmond section. A photo on the restaurant wall shows Giovanni Denino, arms at his side, his wife beside him. There is a Chesterfield cigarettes display in the window; the awning reads "Confectionary Deninos Stationery."

Denino's storefront, early 1900s

"They also made lemon ice," Palma says of her grandparents. "They made bleach, delivered that. You had the egg man who used to come, the bread man."

Carlo, according to regular Sonny Perricone, was a "wild kid but not a bad kid."

"Being around him was an adventure," Perricone recalls in one of the many framed testimonials to Carlo Denino on the restaurant's walls. "They would go to the A&P on the corner of Richmond Avenue and Catherine Street and take fruit which was out in front of the store. I have faint memories of him behind the wheel the wheel of Uncle John's car. He couldn't see over the steering wheel, but he drove anyway."

In 1925, Giovanni opened a pool hall next door. In 1933, with the repeal of Prohibition, he started serving beer; in 1937, he opened a full-scale tavern at Denino's current location, just down the street.

The menu at the time was blue-collar fare—ham and cheese, and salami and cheese, sandwiches. There was something called a "melted" sandwich—just cheese. Scungilli was added in the 1940s.

"We had to fight to add anything to the menu," Mike Burke, Palma's son, says. "He

[Carlo Denino] wanted to keep it simple."

Back then, Port Richmond was a bustling neighborhood with "beautiful shops, beautiful dress stores," according to Palma.

"It was the shopping mecca of Staten Island through the late fifties into the sixties, early seventies," her son explains.

There were Gene's, the Venetian Gardens, and other popular restaurants. Jersey kids would come over the Outerbridge and Bayonne bridges since the drinking age was eighteen in New York State at the time.

At Denino's, Carlo kept chickens in pens behind the building. "My sister Rose hated them," Palma says, laughing. "She would go in, they would peck her on the head."

When Carlo added pizza to the menu in 1951, he "takes Staten Island by surprise," according to the family.

Denino's was not Staten Island's first pizzeria; Lee's Tavern, for one, opened in 1940. But it would become the most famous.

"It was popular right away," Michael says. "I don't think he had any idea how big it would become. He was always slow to act. He didn't want to make a fuss."

Pizza came in two sizes—small, about a dollar; large, $1.25. It was put not in a box but in a bag, the old-fashioned way.

The tavern was close quarters, and pool players "would have to kick the door to the men's room open to take a shot," Michael says, laughing. "Bob the bus driver would be in there, sitting on the toilet, and you'd open the door."

Carlo Denino at the bar in Denino's.

Carlo loved driving his Volkswagen Beetle and good-naturedly threatened the neighborhood kids that if they didn't behave he'd toss them in his oven. He called the meatball/salami sandwich the "60/40" because the meatballs were bigger. On Sundays the old-timers would play bocce in a makeshift court out back. Carlo never drank at the bar. "He would never sit down with the guys," Michael says. "He would never buy drinks."

His conversations, according to his

daughter, Carla, "were short and sweet."

But there was a merry side to the pizza man. Michael says Carlo would race down the Staten Island Expressway and immediately pull over when he'd spot wild mushrooms.

"He called me Carla maybe once in my life," Carla recalls. "It was always Harriet."

"He'd call all the girls Harriet or Grace or whatever," Michael adds. "He'd call all the guys Smitty."

Palma met her future husband in 1968; he was twenty-seven years her senior.

"I don't know whether to call her Sis or Mom," Carla cracks. "There's only eleven years difference in our ages."

Carlo passed away suddenly in 2000; 2,500 people attended the wake at Casey Funeral Home on Slosson Avenue.

"They just kept coming and coming," Palma said, awestruck.

Carlo loved playing golf, and that's how he departed.

"He died on the golf course," Palma says.

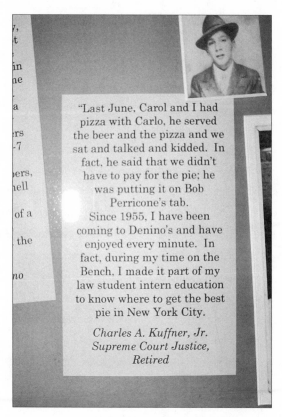

Testimonial on wall of Denino's.

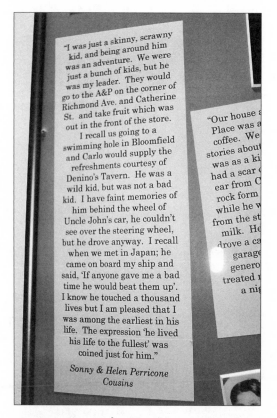

Another memory of Carlo Denino on the wall

"Second hole at Cream Ridge [Golf Club, in New Jersey]," Michael adds.

Carlo Denino is buried at a cemetery overlooking the Richmond County Country Club off Todt Hill Road.

Remembrances fill the walls just inside the entrance of Denino's.

"I lived next door to Carlo's sister V," MaryAnn "Grace" Pandullo wrote. "Every time he would come to visit her and Artie (which was quite often) bringing her many vegetables, he would always pull his car in her driveway and yell out, 'Hey, Grace, you home,' and I would go to the kitchen window and we would have a chat. I miss his voice . . . a gentleman in the true sense of the word."

From Carla: "On my wedding day as I was walking down the aisle, I began to cry. My father turned to me and said, 'Screw the money, Harriet, if you're not sure, we are out of here.' He was the best friend I ever had and he will always be in my heart. I am so proud when people say 'You are just like your father.'"

Michael remembers that his half sister used to be known as "one-punch Carla."

She lived up to the name one night in response to a customer who was not behaving properly. "I knocked him over the pool table," Carla says proudly. "Don't remember who he was."

Aunt Rose, the one who kept getting pecked by the chickens, passed away three years ago. "She was a big flirt," Palma says. "A good-looking guy would come in, she'd say, 'He can put his shoes under my bed.' But she would never fool around."

Dining rooms were added and expanded over the years; seating capacity of the once cozy neighborhood tavern is now 250. The pool tables were eliminated in early 2002. "I think he would be in shock if he saw it," Palma says of her late husband.

Calzones were added to the menu in the 1970s; they were dropped ten years ago. Carlo didn't want salad on the menu; the family added it after he passed. Looking for pasta? You won't find it here. Appetizers include scungilli, fried calamari, and wings. There are half a dozen heroes, including Carlo's "60/40," plus five platters. The rest of the menu is pizza—twenty-plus kinds, including the Garbage Pie, with sausage, meatballs, pepperoni, mushrooms, and onions.

Denino's has used the same cheese, flour, and tomatoes for years; their butcher is Belfiore Meats, on Victory Boulevard. The bread comes from Melone Brothers Bakery. They use Grande cheese for the mozzarella sticks; Polly-O mozzarella for the pizza.

And Port Richmond is now and will forever be home.

"We've never had a problem here," says Michael, a former fireman. "Once or twice we got robbed." He smiles. "One time, some guy squeezed through the fan in the kitchen

FACT:
More pizza is consumed during Super Bowl week than any other week of the year.

from the outside. There was nothing to take."

Carla is waitress/host; Palma does the paperwork. "Hate it with a passion," she says.

"You have to save every single receipt for three years for the sales tax," Michael points out.

They opened a store in Brick, New Jersey, in October 2010. Michael brings five-gallon jugs of New York City water down to that store every day; he doesn't trust the Jersey water.

There are no plans to open any more stores, either in the city or in Jersey.

"You'd have to have someone there," Palma says.

"From the family," her son adds.

The regular pizza has barely changed—thin crust, distinctive homemade sauce, blackened around the edges.

"In Jersey, you can tell who's local and who's from New York," Michael says. "[Jerseyans] would look at this pizza and say, 'It's burnt.'"

Paper plates are used, but just for the pizza.

"We would never be able to keep up," says Palma, thinking of all the dishes that would need to be washed.

"Forget about it," Carla adds.

Old school? You could say so. No credit cards, no delivery, no Sicilian pizza on the menu. Butter was available for the first time in the fall of 2011. It's pleasantly noisy in the dining room, where Michael's son hops from table to table, greeting friends. Informality prevails.

"It's not fine dining, service-wise," Michael explains. "You want a fork—get up and get it yourself."

He Dreams of Pizza

"Some guys dream about making passionate love to a beautiful supermodel. Personally, I dream about digging my face into a mouth-watering slice of New York City pizza."

Jason Feirman may want to amend that statement. Why not dream about making passionate love to a beautiful supermodel—and having a slice afterward?

There is a photo of him, age five, smile on his face, half-eaten pizza on a plate, during a birthday party at Chuck E. Cheese. The smile seemingly has never left his face, at least when it comes to the subject of pizza. Feirman is the guy behind *I Dream of Pizza*. There are scores of one-person pizza blogs out there, but maybe none is more charmingly obsessive than *I Dream of Pizza*.

Jason Feirman.

Most blogs stick to reviews of pizzerias; Feirman tosses in video, the latest pizza news (who knew Scott Ian and Charlie Benanate from heavy metal band Anthrax were such pizza experts?), and reviews of pizzerias from near and far—the five boroughs, of course, but also Pittsburgh, New Haven, Miami, Chicago, Portland, San Francisco, Toronto, and Tel Aviv.

Jason was into pizza at an early age.

"My favorite pie was the Bianca," begins his report on a Tel Aviv pizzeria called The Pizza. "It was essentially a mix of really flavorful cheeses on bread with a touch of olive oil and parsley—a tre formaggi of sorts. So simple, yet so delicious. Six of the nine pies on the menu at The Pizza lack tomato sauce and I think they're better off for it. The House pie and Aglio Olio pie, for example, are very similar, but the tomato sauce takes away from many of the other flavors on the House pie."

When he travels—Israel, Spain, Italy, Argentina in recent years—he is always on the pizza lookout.

"It was clear that Da Michele was not, in fact, worthy of being part of a conversation about the best pizza in Naples," he wrote of a visit to what is Naples's most famous pizzeria. "Many pizzas I ate throughout the week were difficult to dig into with out a knife and fork. But at Da Michele, it was impossible. The pies, and especially the Margherita, were soggy and instantly [fell] apart. The cheese and sauce was uninspiring. The crust was a little bit undercooked."

Feirman grew up in Potomac, Maryland, and fondly recalls Sunday night family trips to Jerry's Subs for pizza, but the bulk of his early pizza experience came at Sbarro's, at a nearby mall.

"Ever since I was a little boy, pizza has always had a special place in my heart," he writes in "Why I Love Pizza," his first full post on *I Dream of Pizza* in November 2008. "From pizza day in the school cafeteria to pizza parties at sleep away camp, there was nothing more exciting than when that cardboard box was opened to reveal a round pie with eight delicious slices waiting to be devoured."

In high school, there was Giuseppe's, in Rockville, Maryland ("so delicious; I stop there whenever I go home").

But his true pizza education didn't start until he moved to New York to attend NYU, where he majored in journalism and psychology. He could "barely walk a block" without hitting a slice joint—Pizza Booth, The Pizzeria, and Ben's, where he ran into Adam Sandler on

Jason Feirman with a pizza maker in Jerusalem.

one visit. He spent a semester studying in Florence, then moved to Manhattan's East Side—which meant a new batch of pizzerias—Nino's, Pizzanini, Two Boots, and others.

In the summer of 2008, after reading a *New York* magazine story listing the best pizza in each borough, Feirman formed a Pizza Club among friends to check out those places, and more. *I Dream of Pizza* was born.

There was no reaction to his first few posts. But when the blog was mentioned in the *New York Times* and the Newark *Star-Ledger*, "things really took off." He started receiving intriguing e-mails—"I'm opening a place in Alabama, if you're ever out here, stop in."

In October 2009, a legendary pizza "meet-up" occurred at Nomad Pizza in Hopewell, New Jersey. Call it the pizza equivalent of the famed mob Apalachin meeting in 1957, minus the guns and gangsters. Feirman met Adam Kuban, founder of the *Slice* pizza blog; Scott Wiener, owner of Scott's Pizza Tours; and other pizza fanatics.

Jason Feirman and
Scott Wiener (left)
at an Italian pizzeria.

"It was the first time I felt part of the pizza community," Feirman says.

In February 2010, he and Wiener pizza-toured Italy; their stops included a Naples pizzeria whose owner once made a butternut squash pizza for the pope.

In September 2010, Feirman added a new element to his New York pizza repertoire—the NYC Pizza Run, where participants scamper 2.5 miles while stopping to eat three slices along the way. The 2011 Pizza Run attracted a hundred runners; one newspaper headline read, "Three Laps, Hold the Anchovies."

Feirman held a pizza party on his apartment rooftop in the summer of 2011; he hopes to host more in the future.

Would he ever open his own pizzeria?

"Unlikely," replies the blogger, now in the MBA program at Columbia. "It would have to fill some void geographically. But there's no great kosher pizza place. So much is so bad."

His favorite pizza toppings are caramelized onions and sautéed mushrooms. One item he would never put on a pizza: anchovies ("disgusting"). His "go-to" pizzeria is South Brooklyn Pizza, but his all-time favorite is Di Fara in Brooklyn.

"It's the experience—you wait in line and watch [Domenico DeMarco] make pizza. The basil comes from Israel. The sauce is great. One of my favorite parts is when he pours on the olive oil."

In the documentary *The Best Thing I Ever Done* by Margaret Emily MacKenzie, Feirman calls Di Fara's not only the best pizza but the best meal he's eaten anywhere.

He ranks Brooklyn as the best pizza borough. Manhattan is second. Trying to find good pizza midtown and uptown? Don't.

"Ninety-nine percent of the good [Manhattan] pizza is south of 14th Street," he maintains. "The pizza world is revolving around downtown."

It wasn't long ago that pizza bloggers were considered like gnats—easily ignored or swatted away. Now restaurants are paying them attention.

"Five years ago, restaurants were reaching out to the *New York Times*," Feirman says. "Now they're also reaching out to bloggers."

Tripping in Bushwick

Considering all the praise that's been heaped on Roberta's in Bushwick, you may expect a velvet-carpeted entrance with massive stone lions, white-gloved parking attendants, and a hushed, chandelier-lit dining room.

Roberta's entrance is far from grand.

What you get is a brick wall covered in graffiti, a chipped, faded sign above a battered green door, and a thick black curtain you sweep aside to enter the dining room, which will remind you more of a beer hall than what the *New York Times* called "one of the more extraordinary restaurants in the United States."

Within the sprawling complex are two dozen hops crates from an old Brooklyn brewery used as flower planters, an Internet radio station fashioned from two shipping containers, spit roasters and mobile pizza ovens, a garden, and the army tent that serves as the year-round tiki bar.

"People come by, they're tripping," Chris Parachini is saying. "This used to be an old junkyard."

Chris Parachini, co-owner,
Roberta's, Bushwick.

It is a cold, miserable day in the bleak neighborhood Roberta's calls home. You could easily walk right past the place and not notice the entrance; it's practically lost in a storm of graffiti. The story here is not just the presence of a highly acclaimed pizzeria/restaurant in beaten-down Bushwick but the DIY spirit—driven if not downright maniacal—that led to its opening.

It all begins with Parachini, a thirty-nine-year-old Jersey native who flips up the hood on his green pullover when it comes time to shoot his picture. If he looks more like street person than restaurant owner, well then, so be it.

He was not the best student in Union City, New Jersey, where he grew up, nor the best behaved.

"I cut class a lot. I got into situations where I was asked to leave every year," he says cryptically.

In his late teens, he "meandered all over the country," ending up in California, days of endless summer and surfing. He moved to Williamsburg, Brooklyn, in 2003. His dad owned several restaurants, including the Players Club in Hackensack, New Jersey. Chris worked as a bartender there, eventually getting fired.

"It took me five years, but I did it," he says, grinning.

Bartending was "easy money," even if he lived "like a vampire." But he became tired of the work and grew "hungry to do something." Opening a restaurant seemed like it would be "more fun."

It wouldn't be in suddenly-happening Williamsburg, though. He didn't like the scene. "Too many baby strollers," he says, smiling. "I didn't want to see baby strollers."

He moved to Bushwick, which was "like moving out to the country. It was without trees. It was cheap. It was lawless, unwatched by the police."

He and his brother shared a floor in an old factory building.

The turning point in his life came over Thanksgiving in 2006. Parachini visited legendary pizza joint Frank Pepe's in New Haven for the first time.

"I was kind of moved. Everybody was having a good time. It was lively, unpretentious. It felt so right."

Shanti Carson,
a waitress at Roberta's.

Back in New York, he ran into Brandon Hoy, a friend from his bartending days; the two met at a bar and talked restaurant.

"I asked him, 'Do you have any money? I don't have anything,'" Parachini recalls.

Hoy gave him $13,000 in savings, just enough to pay the deposit and first month's rent on a building on Moore Street in Bushwick. The two begin to transform the space, using materials that didn't exactly come from Home Depot.

Parachini admits he lifted a lot of brick from demolished buildings, loading up vans at night.

"It's funny what you do when you don't have any money," he observes.

Tables were built from old doors bought for $5 upstate.

"We built everything ourselves," Parachini explains. "It seemed really stupid to go out and buy stuff."

In 2007, Carlo Mirarchi, former chef at Good World restaurant in Chinatown and a friend of Hoy's, joined the team, adding $30,000 to the pot.

The restaurant opened on January 3, 2008—with no heat, gas, or hot water.

"We had no money," Parachini says. "No gas, no hot water for six months. If the health department had walked in at any moment we would have been shut down."

Space heaters provided heat, and cooking was done over cassette propane burners placed atop the useless gas range. A toaster oven or two provided backup. At the beginning, the menu included pizza, charcuterie/cheese plates, and pork chops cooked in the wood-fired oven.

Pizza oven, Roberta's.

And that means you.

Eighty people were invited to an opening party; four hundred showed up. "We were busy from the get-go," Parachini says. "The neighborhood was stoked."

A *New York Times* review that March was positive, but Parachini was disappointed. "We wanted to stay under the radar," he says.

In 2008, Patrick Martins, who started Slow Food USA, pitched a food-themed Internet radio station. Heritage Radio Network, built into two repurposed twenty-foot shipping containers, began at Roberta's in March 2009.

The shows, broadcast live, can be downloaded as podcasts or RSS feeds. Programs include "Hot Grease," about sustainability and the local food movement; "Burning Down the House," "a weekly discourse on all things built, destroyed, admired, and despised"; "Beer Sessions Radio"; "The Food Seen," about the lives of chefs and the inner workings of kitchens; and "Cutting the Curd," about cheese.

A garden was added out back; Roberta's employs a full-time gardener, Melissa Metrick.

"We learned what we should be growing and should not be growing," Parachini explains. "It took a lot of time to realize it wouldn't make sense to grow heirloom tomatoes. It made sense to grow borage and greens. A lot of this stuff cost $10 a pound [from suppliers]."

One day, Alice Waters of Chez Panisse fame paid a visit and wrote a check for $1,000.

By this time, Roberta's was on everyone's radar; Sam Sifton called it "one of the more extraordinary restaurants in the United States" in an August 2011 review.

Roberta's backyard
is off-limits.

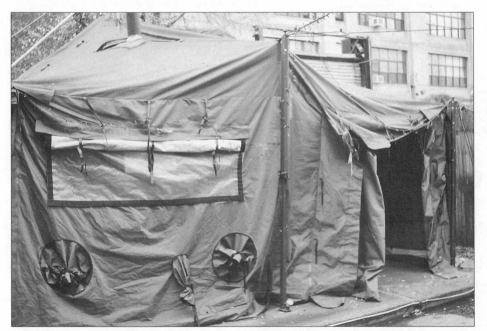

A former army tent is now
the tiki bar at Roberta's.

A tiki bar was added to the sprawling complex. It's nothing more than an army tent bought for $100 at an army surplus store and heated by a wood-burning stove that burns red and white oak from Pennsylvania.

"It's been through hurricanes, nor'easters," Parachini says proudly.

The old body shop next door was acquired and turned into offices, a conference room, a wine storage room, and a state-of-the-art kitchen.

"This is going to be the production and catering kitchen," says Parachini, leading a tour over the sound of drills. "We don't have enough prep space."

The new space will enable Roberta's to host tasting dinners where twelve guests "will get the meals of their lives," according to Parachini.

That space became Blanca in summer 2012. The $180-a-person tasting menu "might be the single most impossible reservation in town," *TimeOut New York* reported.

"When you come in here in three months, something will be different," Parachini says. "The restaurant business is the theater business. When you make a new restaurant, it's like making a new record. You get to be creative. You live or die by the performance you put on."

Chalk message board
at Roberta's.

The in-house bakery makes bread for the restaurant and for outside accounts; the head baker is Melissa Weller.

For months, the pizza itself was a work in progress. The initial crust was more crackery; Parachini started "messing with different hydration levels and other things" to produce a pizza that was "supple on the inside, crispy enough on the outside."

In the restaurant's opening year, things were more informal than they are now. Customers would hang out in the kitchen, knocking off six-packs of beer.

Roberta's uses Stumptown
Coffee Roasters, Brooklyn.

"It was wild, it was cool, it was like a proper neighborhood restaurant," Parachini recalls.

Except that the neighborhood wasn't so proper.

"This street was a very popular street for insurance jobs. They'd burn cars once or twice a week. The street was dead and dangerous. There was nothing in this neighborhood. Nobody thought we'd make money."

The website, like the restaurant and its founder, is pretense-free. There are menus, a monthly calendar, catering and group dining info, and nine photos. There are no fawning restaurant reviews; the section headlined "Press" is simply an e-mail for press inquiries.

Did Parachini have any doubts he would succeed? "I don't think so, man. We had done so much with so little. Failure wasn't an option, and we were doing something no one else was doing."

He describes Roberta's as "the sum of a lot of parts. A living thing that has its own personality. It's in constant motion. It's not an academic course; it's an exercise in living good, feeling good.

"We've never known where the f—— we're headed," he adds. "You go down the path, see where you end up. The world is in chaos. We're committed to making it the best we can."

Going Mobile

Mike Vallario, big Yankees fan, tries to smack the ball out of the park with his first swing.

"There's more better pizza in Staten Island than the rest of the city," brags the fifty-one-year-old owner of Valducci's pizza truck.

You can hear the Bronx cheers go up from Manhattan and Brooklyn, but Vallario is from Staten Island, and his truck and former restaurant started there, so pardon his enthusiasm.

New York City is home to scores of gourmet food trucks; oddly, there are just five regularly operating pizza trucks as of this writing: Valducci's, Eddie's Pizza Truck, the Pizza Truck of New York, Jiannetto's, and Pizza Luca.

But industry observers see plenty of potential. Food trucks in general are hot—there are lively gourmet truck scenes in Austin, Los Angeles, San Francisco, Washington, D.C., and, of course, New York City—but pizza so far has taken a back seat. You can find Mexican, Cuban, Korean, Indian, ice cream, burgers, and much more on trucks, but the world's most popular food? Not so much.

PMQ Pizza Magazine, citing estimates that 10 percent of the top two hundred national restaurant chains would "have food trucks on the streets by 2012," said pizza had "the potential to lead the pack."

FACT:
The average pizzeria uses about fifty-five pizza boxes a day.

Mike Vallario, owner of Valducci's Pizza Truck.

In New York City, at least, pizza has a long way to go before even catching up to the pack. Which makes the appearance of a pizza truck anywhere in the city a welcome sight. Eddie's Pizza Truck hit the streets of Manhattan in June 2010; it gets its name from Eddie's Pizza in New Hyde Park. The truck, owned by Derek Kaye, is known for its 270-calorie thin-crust bar pies; no slices are available.

Eddie's Pizza Truck, downtown.

The dough is par-baked at the restaurant; sauce and toppings are added at the truck, where the dough is cooked the rest of the way. The most popular pizzas are the Eddie's Favorite (sausage, meatballs, pepperoni, mushrooms, peppers, onions) and the Hot Chicken Pizza.

Eddie's has made several guest appearances

on HBO's show *Entourage*. In one episode, Turtle has Eddie's pizzas shipped to L.A.; cast members have worn Eddie's T-shirts on several episodes. Another high point: Eddie's catered an Alicia Keys/Swizz Beatz party.

The truck, built by Shanghai Stainless in Brooklyn, is nicely fitted: air-conditioning, two ovens, retractable remote-controlled awning, surround-sound music, and a twenty-

six-inch LCD TV. The truck shuttles between the World Financial Center, midtown, the Upper East Side, and elsewhere.

Asked how many places the truck has been parked, Debbie Jones, Eddie's director of operations, replies, "Lots! We look on Twitter to see where other trucks are, and we don't park there when they do."

The Eddie's and Valducci's trucks are never closer than a dozen or so blocks from each other, and their pizzas are worlds apart

Debbie Jones, manager, Eddie's Pizza Truck.

anyway. Valducci's truck started with the pizzeria of the same name, which opened in 1989 in Eltingville, on Staten Island's south shore. The name is a contraction of the Vallario family name and his great-grandmother's last name—Ducci.

Vallario rented a storefront that had seen a succession of pizzerias. He knew the space because he ran a real estate business right next door. He bought the pizzeria, then opened a family-style Italian restaurant a half mile away.

9/11 remembrance, Valducci's Pizza Truck.

He would eventually sell both restaurants and concentrate on the truck, finding a choice location at the corner of Wall and Water streets. His brother Pete ran the business for the most part between 1999 and 2007.

Then came 9/11. Several days after the terror attacks, the brothers were allowed to move the truck to the corner of Vesey Street and the West Side Highway, a block from the smoldering ruins. For four days, Vallario, his brothers Pete and Danny, and friend Kevin McLeary made pizza around the clock for cops, firefighters, EMTs, and others.

Valducci's
Pizza Truck.

"It was the scariest time of my life," Vallario says. "It was satisfying—we got a lot of 'glad you're here,' but it was a scary place to be."

Vallario sold the truck to one of his workers, then decided to buy another truck, a 1997 Grumman Olson that had been used as a laundry pickup truck. Location is everything in the pizza truck business, and Vallario found a good one at the corner of 52nd Street and Park Avenue, where Valducci's can be found during lunchtime. Then it moves downtown, to Sixth Avenue and 24th Street, for dinner, and moves one more time, for a late-night pizza shift in the meatpacking district. Make that well into the morning; the truck stays open until 5 A.M.

Eddie's Pizza Truck boxes.

What does it cost to operate a pizza truck? The annual permit from the city costs $300. Vallario shells out $600 a month to store the truck at a commissary. He won't say how much money he makes, but he's sure not making it from tourists.

"Tourists don't buy pizza, not on a truck," he explains. "They'll spend $4 on a hot dog or pretzel, but not pizza."

One of his workers shows up, and Vallario delivers three boxes of slices to a nearby bank. He returns ten minutes later. How far away is the bank?

"Right there," he replies, pointing to the Chase Bank entrance not twenty feet away. "They couldn't come out here and pick it up?"

"They give me so much [in tips], I can deliver it."

For the first few months here, Vallario sold just a plain Sicilian slice. Now slices include ricotta and meatball; peppers and sausage; vodka; and oreganata.

Sausage and pepperoni pizza, Eddie's Pizza Truck.

He says his best pizza is a round plain cheese, but he doesn't serve it on the truck; he's "saving" it for a brick-oven pizzeria he hopes to open in Chelsea.

His "old-fashioned" tomato slice is my favorite slice here. Fresh out of the oven, it's a bubbling steaming red sea of sauce.

A familiar face appears at the window. It's a homeless man who regularly picks up a free slice from Vallario. "I've always been big on charities," the latter explains.

His advice to prospective truck owners? "Get ready to work hard" and "You better make some good sauce."

His sauce is based on his mom's, with some tweaks from her son. The vodka sauce is pretty much his.

"It may be the best vodka sauce you'll ever have," Vallario says. Then the pizza man smiles. "I better shut up."

Lombardi's

Pizza history, at least in this country, begins with Lombardi's.

Not only was the Spring Street pizzeria the first in New York City, it was the training ground for several legendary pizza makers—John Sasso of John's on Bleecker Street, Anthony Pero of Totonno's in Coney Island, and Pasquale "Patsy" Lancieri, founder of Patsy's in East Harlem.

John Brescio, co-owner of Lombardi's.

Gennaro Lombardi, who learned how to make pizza as a kid in Naples, came to the United States at age fourteen, working as a baker in Brooklyn. A go-getter, he bought a bakery when he was just seventeen. He sold thin Neapolitan-type pizzas. Business was good, and in 1905 Lombardi acquired the first license to sell pizza in New York City.

Plaque in Lombardi's for being inducted into the Pizza Hall of Fame.

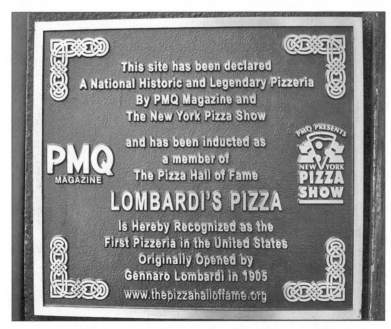

This site has been declared A National Historic and Legendary Pizzeria By PMQ Magazine and The New York Pizza Show

PMQ MAGAZINE

and has been inducted as a member of The Pizza Hall of Fame

PMQ PRESENTS

NEW YORK **PIZZA SHOW**

LOMBARDI'S PIZZA

Is Hereby Recognized as the First Pizzeria in the United States Originally Opened by Gennaro Lombardi in 1905

www.thepizzahalloffame.org

There is no doubt in John Brescio's mind that Lombardi's was not only the first pizzeria in the city but the first in the country. Asked whether someone else could have been making pizza in New York before Gennaro Lombardi, Brescio is quick to reply.

"No," he says. "No, no, no."

The sixty-three-year-old Brescio is co-owner of Lombardi's with Gerry Lombardi, grandson of Gennaro. A 1905 photo on the wall shows Lombardi—chiseled face, wavy hair, blue shirt, white waiter-type jacket over black pants—and Anthony Pero standing on the pizzeria's wooden steps.

The same photo, not surprisingly, is on the wall at Totonno's in Coney Island, which Pero founded. "Pizzeria Napoletana," reads the storefront lettering at Lombardi's original store. Cans of tomatoes six, seven rows high form a window display. A small sign advertises "Friday Night Casino Girls" at a nearby show hall. A pushcart filled with bananas is parked out front.

"This whole neighborhood was Italian," Brescio said. "Most of the people who lived around here worked in factories in SoHo."

Lombardi's was originally a grocery store but started offering food for the factory workers in SoHo. Most could not afford a whole pizza, so it was sold by the piece, several pennies each. The pizzas were wrapped in brown paper and tied with a string so workers could take it with them.

Anthony Pero (left) and Gennaro Lombardi (right) outside Lombardi's storefront in 1905.

The Lombardi family in the upstairs dinner room.

85

At the beginning, Lombardi made just one kind of pizza—a thin-crust Neapolitan style with local mozzarella and Italian tomatoes. Toppings did not come along until much later.

Lombardi, an immigrant, was only too happy to help those who came after him.

"Here was the kind of person he was," Brescio says. "Any person coming over from Italy, he would get them a job, give them a room upstairs."

Brescio's father and Gennaro Lombardi were friends, and the pizzeria became a hangout for the neighborhood kids.

"My father would leave us with Gennaro and Jerry," Brescio recalls. "We would play there all day. He would throw dough balls at us and we would throw them back. Plenty of times we would hit him in the head with a dough ball."

After Lombardi passed away, his son, John, and later grandson, Jerry, took over.

Vintage advertising, Lombardi's.

The 1950s saw the emergence of pizza as an American food staple, largely due to GIs returning home and craving the pizza they had enjoyed in Italy.

In the 1960s and 1970s, Lombardi's became a "high-end" restaurant, according to Brescio, counting Jackie Onassis among its customers. But the pizzeria closed in 1984, a victim of a flagging economy. In 1994, Brescio and Jerry Lombardi reopened Lombardi's down the street, at 32 Spring Street.

The pizza Gennaro Lombardi made—mozzarella and Italian tomatoes—can be found at Lombardi's today, with a choice of sweet Italian sausage, homemade meatballs, wild fresh mushrooms, Citterio pancetta, and other toppings. The only other pizza available is a white. There is no Sicilian or chicken or Grandma or any other kind of pizza. Brescio's favorite pizza: fresh mushrooms and roasted red peppers.

Asked to describe Lombardi's pizza, he offers this: "Crusty on the outside, light and airy on the inside, and the cheese and toppings stay moist. That's what makes a great pie."

He reveals where he gets his "beautiful fresh plum tomatoes"—Lucky's Tomatoes, from Florida—but not his pepperoni.

"I'm not going to say where I get it. It doesn't leave a puddle [in cooking]. It leaves a nice crunch when you bite it.

"I could use canned mushrooms—90 percent of pizzerias do," he adds. "I'd rather close than use canned."

Picture of the old—
and still working—oven
at Lombardi's.

He uses about six hundred pounds of coal a day for his oven. Up to four hundred pizzas are made every day.

Several critics have sneered that only "tourists" go to Lombardi's these days, but on my recent visit several regulars—all New Yorkers—greeted Brescio warmly. Later, Brescio would say hello to a group of visitors from Italy, one of whom thought he might be a distant relation of Gennaro Lombardi.

The ever-packed Spring Street pizzeria has seen its share of celebs, Jack Nicholson among the most notable. "That girl Fergie [from the Black Eyed Peas] was here," Brescio explains. "I don't like to bother anybody; I don't go up for a picture. If they want me to come over, I'll come over."

There is a photo of one customer and his monkey; the two would pop in twice a week, at a time when monkeys, apparently, were allowed in restaurants. The monkey's choice of topping: pepperoni.

In 2005, on the pizzeria's hundredth anniversary, Lombardi's sold pizzas for 25 cents.

"One lady complained, 'Why didn't you roll back the prices on the soda?'" Brescio says, laughing.

The Pizza Self-Sufficiency Center

The sauce-red awning on Grand Street provides a clue that Mark Bello's pizza school is not some stuffy classroom where students speak in hushed tones, and only when spoken to.

"Pizza a Casa," proclaims the sign. "Pizza Self-Sufficiency Center."

All you tired, huddled, frustrated pizza masses yearning to be free from your kitchen, where the pizza never comes out right—take a course at PSSC.

Pizza a Casa is one-stop shopping for all your pizza-making needs.

"Do you have dough issues?" Bello asks a student before the start of his four-hour pizza school.

His students tonight are from New York, New Jersey, Ohio, Oklahoma, the Netherlands, Spain, and Costa Rica. Some are accomplished cooks, others rank beginners. For the next four hours, they'll get a pizza crash course. And learn all sorts of things. Fresh dough can be kept five to six days in the fridge; dough can be frozen for up to six months. Never use a rolling pin, never throw your dough. Don't chop your basil; snip it, with an herb scissors. Pre-roast your vegetables, normally full of water, so the top of the pizza "doesn't turn into a swimming pool."

"Bad pizza," says a sign on the wall, "should not happen to good people."

For Bello, it's been a long strange trip from Mount Sinai Hospital, where he was born, to Westchester County and Short Hills, New Jersey, where he grew up, to the big city.

"There are those who shopped at the mall and those who worked at the mall," he says of his days as a student at Millburn (New Jersey) High School. "I worked at the mall. Gap."

He attended college at Washington University in St. Louis, majoring in fine arts. Then it was on to Chicago, where he majored in sculpture at the School of the Art Institute of Chicago. To pay his bills, he opened a furniture store in the Windy City, Right-On Futon.

Pizza options in the Second City, he says, were two: deep dish and "bad chain delivery pizzeria."

What was a New York boy to do? Freeze slices from Lombardi's and bring them home on the plane.

Bello started making and perfecting pizzas at home, and when he moved back to New York in 2006, he gave pizza classes at the Astor Center, Whole Foods, Murray's Cheese, even in his apartment. Pizza a Casa opened in April 2010 to immediate acclaim; the *Village Voice* named his pizza one of the city's three best, even though you couldn't buy it anywhere.

"Tonight's class," he tells his dozen students, "will be condensed to six action-packed pages."

Mark Bello, founder of Pizza a Casa.

The "curriculum" takes novice pizza makers through eleven steps, from "Wash Your Hands" ("If you like lovely scented hand creams, unless they are something like delicious garlic flavor, it is imperative that you wash them off well before working with dough") to "Set Aside to Rise," "Dress Up Your Crust," and "Cut, Serve, Bow, and Eat!"

Consider the Pizza a Casa phone number your "dough emergency hotline," Bello tells the class.

A student's egg pizza.

Students each make five pizzas from scratch. In theory, anyway, because there will always be someone—say, a writer doing a book on pizza—who will completely botch one ball of dough and thus make only four pizzas (in the interest of fairness, said writer brought nonbotched slices to the office the next day, and received rave reviews).

"Pizza making is part sense, part sensibility," Bello continues.

Did Jane Austen make pizza?

Actually, pizza making is easier than you think—if you follow the pizza sensei's directions and use quality ingredients.

His fresh mozzarella is from Alleva Dairy, farmstead cheese from Saxelby Cheese-mongers, meat toppings from Jeffrey's Meat Market, sweet clams from Hai Thanh Seafood, pans from Bari Equipment.

For sauce, Bello uses La Bella San Marzano Passata di Pomodoro. His pizza cutter? He won't use anything but a Dexter-Russell P177A. Viking donated a $6,000 oven, plus mixers and other supplies. Bello designed the space—kitchen, central table, faux brick walls, TV screen. Don't forget the mirror ball in the corner.

This is all you need to make great pizza: three and a half cups of unbleached all-purpose flour, one and a half cups of water, a packet of Fleischmann's active dry yeast, a pinch of sugar, a teaspoon of extra-virgin olive oil, a teaspoon of sea salt.

Oh, and follow directions.

"I respectfully ask you to play with your dough," Bello says at one point. "Work it."

The dough will be ready in just forty-five minutes; in pizzerias, it's known as "emergency dough"—when you've got to have dough quick.

Don't worry if your neighbor's container of working yeast has more bubbles than yours. Knead, dust with semolina flour, knead some more.

As students wait for their dough to develop, Bello makes five pizzas—a margherita, a smoked mozzarella, a potato and rosemary, a white pizza, and one with truffle oil and honey. Standing nearby is girlfriend Jenny Phillips, his "pizza traffic controller," who will later coordinate the flow of student-made pizza in the oven.

Jenny Phillips is the "pizza traffic controller" at the school.

"You don't need a fancy oven to get results," says Bello, breaking out a nifty infrared thermometer to check the oven's temperature.

He recently made pizza for a radio show in a $99 Cuisinart tabletop oven. How did it turn out? "Unbelievable."

The Pizza Self-Sufficiency Center lives up to its name. Shelves are stocked with every imaginable pizza-making product. Mozzarella cheese-making kits, natural sea salt from Italy, "genuine Italian dried pine seeds," kid-safe pizza cutters, instant-read pocket thermometers, garlic peelers, baking stones, even peppermill holsters.

Sign inside Pizza a Casa.

A *Mad* magazine cover on the wall shows Alfred E. Neuman rolling a gigantic pizza out of a shop. There are photos of Bello from his Chicago days. Class is held to the beat of an eclectic house mix—Gladys Knight to Flock of Seagulls to Judas Priest.

The dough making over, Bello passes around samples of cow's milk mozzarella from Alleva; he prefers the fior di latte to more expensive bufala, which he finds "very, very creamy; your pizza ends up soupy." He once tried some domestic bufala from Wisconsin; it tasted like "stinky provolone."

Time for a pizza horror story. Once he and his friend Neil made pizzas for a hundred people at a boat party. Neil—what was he thinking?—added three times the normal amount of oil.

"I've never tasted ceiling tile," Bello recalls, "but I think that was as close as I'll come to trying it."

Melissa Knific is a study in concentration at Pizza a Casa.

Sign on wall at Pizza a Casa.

Carsten Nordsieck happily bites into a slice at Pizza a Casa.

He's given classes to private and corporate clients, "fancy cosmetic companies," even a group from Home Depot ("Their top brass was in town looking for interesting things to do"). When he acquires a liquor license, he'll host dinner parties at Pizza a Casa. Not bad for a futon store owner from Chicago.

When this class is over, students at Pizza a Casa will have made 6,926 pizzas since opening night. As class finally wraps up around 11 P.M., student Mary Ellen Knific surveys the flour-dusted, oil-streaked, vegetable-strewn aftermath. "Can I clean my station?" she asks Phillips.

"No," she replies, laughing. "We'll take care of that."

It's Italian for Scooter

The Leaning Tower of Pisa had nothing on Mathieu Palombino's leaning pizza restaurant.

Palombino, a blue-eyed Belgian who came to this country without any knowledge of English, opened Motorino in Williamsburg, Brooklyn, in 2008 to much acclaim. The *New York Times*'s Sam Sifton went so far as to call it the city's "best pizza."

But the building was doomed. It apparently had started to lean, to the right, in the mid-1990s and only worsened. The landlord hired an architect in April 2011 to stabilize the building, but it was too late. In August 2011, the city shut down Motorino, which had been covered in scaffolding for several months while a crew worked on the structure, for good.

"The stupidity [of the landlord] was a force we were not able to overcome," Palombino said at the time.

These days, everything is on firmer ground. His East Village outpost of Motorino remains one of the city's top pizza destinations. The Bowery Diner, his take on the classic fifties diner, opened in 2012. He also bought a $1.025 million condo in Brooklyn. He hopes to reopen Motorino in Williamsburg someday.

He apologizes for being late to the interview, but there's a good explanation.

"Today we just found out we are having our second baby," he says, eyes alight.

No one in the restaurant world, began a piece in *New York* magazine, "has followed a career path quite like Mathieu Palombino's. First it was all Bouley tasting menus. Then came butter-poached lobsters at Cello followed by salt-crusted pink snappers at BLT Fish. And after that? Margherita pizzas and meatballs at Motorino. Now, with the opening of the Bowery Diner, the Belgian-born, Michelin-starred chef is turning his attention to blue-plate specials, eggs over easy, and whiskeys down."

Actually, the path was interesting well before that.

Mathieu Palombino, owner of Motorino, Manhattan.

Born in Belgium to an Italian father and French mother, he remembers "the beautiful countryside of farms and cows" in his native country.

"I love Belgium. Little country. People are a certain way. Beautiful summer. Rainy the rest of the time. But I wanted to come to New York, like millions of people."

When fourteen, he attended French cooking school. "I figured I wasn't going to be a surgeon. I was attracted by the cooks, the knives, attracted by the idea of working in teams."

In his third year of school, he left. "I wasn't a good student. It was too slow for me. The outside was the real world."

He landed a job at Le Madrigal, a prestigious French restaurant in Paris. "First you learn how to store onions and watercress and potatoes, then you learn how to cook those potatoes." Other duties included driving a van to pick up groceries and meats for the restaurant.

Palombino worked at Le Madrigal until he was nineteen, then moved to Brussels, sleeping at a friend's apartment. He worked at another acclaimed restaurant—Bonsoir Clara, on rue Antoine Dansaert. It was a time of "hard work, hard partying."

Stricken with wanderlust, he took a train to Italy and found another restaurant job, "but my brother turned my mind around. . . . He convinced me to go to New York."

So he did; his first job, at a Belgian bistro in Manhattan, was "the only place I could work; it was French-owned, I couldn't speak English."

His English improved, and so did his positions at a succession of celebrated restaurants—Cello, Boulez, BLT Fish.

"By 2007, I thought I was understanding New York business," he says. "It was time not to work for someone else."

The opportunity came in pizza. He fell in love with Grimaldi's and a cult pizzeria on East 12th Street in the East Village. The name of the place was Una Pizza Napoletano, and when owner A. W. Mangieri moved to San Francisco, Palombino moved in. The Williamsburg Motorino was already open, so when the pizza restaurant collapsed, Palombino's world didn't.

His previous culinary experience didn't help much when it came to making pizza, so Palombino traveled to California and Naples, where he picked up tips and ate "a maximum of pizza."

"I know how it is to perfect things. I knew I was going to do that to my pizza," he explains.

He experimented constantly with dough and crusts and toppings.

"I was breathing pizza night and day. Changing the crust. Fine-tuning the dough. I tried every single fermentation process, every single way to make dough. I had to go to the doctor [at one point]. I was breathing so much flour, I was sick." He smiles. "I was like a mad scientist. I was crazy."

The mad scientist turns almost mystical when he starts talking about dough making, for him the most important part of the pizza process.

"This is life for pizza dough," he says, his hands forming an imaginary ball. "It is born, it has a peak, it dies. You flatten the dough ball, it goes into the oven at a specific time. People said, 'No one is making it like you, nobody is making it so complicated.'"

Even if he's not quite the mad scientist of his early days, he still treats dough making as something sacred. He makes it not at Motorino but at a Brooklyn bakery. "I ferment differently," he says, not wishing to reveal more. He looks around his small restaurant, with its tiny kitchen. "I need more space."

He buys imported cheese through a Brooklyn shop; it comes straight from the airport to Palombino.

Motorino itself may come as a surprise to the first-timer. Anyone expecting a hushed cathedral of pizza, with waiters speaking in reverential tones, will be disappointed. Instead of the usual clutter of clichéd prints and photos on the wall, there is a bicycle wheel and a worn pizza peel. A fax machine is perched on a shelf. The house soundtrack leaps all over the music spectrum. Tom Petty one moment, soothing R&B the next.

Bicycle wheel on wall of Motorino.

Metal chairs—call them lawn chairs for a Riviera summer home—serve as furniture.

It is 2:30 on a Friday afternoon, and the place is packed.

"I didn't bring the Neapolitan pizza to New York," Palombino is saying. "But Motorino definitely started the renaissance. Keste, Co.—they all came after me. The press embraced us right away. The *New York Times* said 'best pizza in New York.' That's a big statement."

Unlike some other high-profile pizzeria owners—who either claim never to have eaten pizza elsewhere or say why would they, their pizza is better—Palombino is quick to praise the competition. He loves the pizzas at Co. and Paulie Gee's.

Palombino in a lighter moment.

"I like [L&B] Spumoni Gardens. Get a slice. Yeah, it's not made from the best flour but it's so good. Everybody eats there."

Lucali's three-cheese pizza? "The best pizza I have eaten in my life. Big chunks of Parmesan. [Mark Iacono's] pies are so good because the flavors are very Italian."

"I go to [Anna] Maria's on Bedford Avenue [Brooklyn]. Joe's [on Carmine in the Village] is an amazing place."

The flagging economy has been "a good thing for me and a bad thing for fine-dining restaurants. All these fancy restaurants started to suffer. Everyone started to eat pizza again. You could eat much cheaper. It is cool, no?"

His "big cool diner" is open, and another Motorino is on the way. His next move? Opening a slice joint somewhere.

"We're missing slice joints," he says. "That's something I'm going to get my hands on. Throw $3 across the counter, walk out with a great slice."

No Pizza Box Is Safe

You could say every true New Yorker is a pizza obsessive. Some take it to the outer limits. We're talking about pizza bloggers, God bless their cholesterol-spiking souls.

Brooks Jones, a filmmaker, writes the blog *Pizza Commander*.

Colin Hagendorf, who does the *Slice Harvester* blog, visited 362 slice joints in Manhattan in two and a half years.

Every October, Sean Taylor (31daysofpizza.com) celebrates National Pizza Month by eating a slice a day, each at a different pizzeria.

There are blogs the likes of *Pizza Maniac, Pizza Slayer, Pizza Goon*.

Shirley Chow somehow stands out, and not because of her food-friendly name. Outwardly serene, she is quietly maniacal when it comes to her collection.

We're not talking "strange" pillows, even though she collects those.

Pizza boxes.

"These bloggers take all this time to write wonderful stories online," she says over pizza at Adrienne's pizzabar in Manhattan. "I just take pictures of pizza boxes."

The Murray Hill resident posts photos of pizza boxes on her website, photosofpizzaboxes.com. She's the first to admit she doesn't have a huge collection of pizza boxes; there's only room for so many in her small apartment.

She doesn't collect any old boxes, though; it's about quality, not quantity. Ninety-five percent of the boxes out there look like they rolled off the same pizza box assembly line—same square box, same slogans—"Made with the Freshest Ingredients," "From Your Favorite Local Pizzeria," and "Delicious Pizza!"

Chow is a searcher, a discoverer, of pizza box art. The monstrous artichoke on the Artichoke Basille's Pizza box. The red-ink drawing of the storefront at Arturo's on West Houston Street. The simple elegance of the box from Best Pizza in Williamsburg—"Best Pizza" in red letters, the phone number, and that's it.

FACT:
There are a dozen or more pizza-related "holidays," including National Pizza Month (October), National Pizza Day (February), National Cheese Pizza Day (September 5), National Pizza Party Day (May 18), National Pizza with Everything Except Anchovies Day (November 12), and, well, you get the idea. The days are the creation of various trade associations and public relations firms.

Shirley Chow,
pizza box collector.

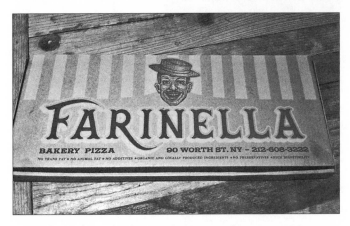

The Farinella box, with its
carnival-barker-like logo.

The curious-looking chap on the Farinella box—he looks more carnival barker than pizza maker—and the stock-ticker-like words at the bottom—"No Trans Fat. No Animal Fat. Organic and Locally Produced Ingredients. High Digestibility."

"I always get a bit tickled with excitement when I come across a rectangular box," Chow says. "I also enjoy the efficiency of triangle boxes for slices, too."

Born in Taiwan, she came to this country as a child. One of her "proudest" memories was a fifth-grade pizza party. She made quick work of five slices. Impressive, even for a kid.

Every summer, she'd visit her aunts and uncles in Washington State, where Godfather's Pizza became a favorite. "They had the most amazing taco and cheeseburger pizzas," she confesses. "Definitely not gourmet, but I was a kid!"

Today, she is public relations manager at 2U Inc., which partners with colleges and universities to deliver selective degree programs online to students globally. Chow started her pizza box blog in November 2009. "It was a long time before anyone noticed it existed," she says sheepishly.

A Twitter account and an interview on *Slice* changed all that. Now it's reached the point where pizzerias will send her photos of their boxes.

Her friends know of her weakness for pizza; for her thirty-first birthday, they prepared toppings in advance (halal chicken and rice, taco, halal lamb, Korean barbecue, cheese and tomatoes) and brought them to Little Italy pizzeria on Union Square, where the toppings were added to pizza.

The curator of the Web's only online pizza box museum rates each pizzeria she visits—not just the box but the pizza itself. Only 4 of her 150-plus entries to date have received a five-box rating and a five-pizza rating: Joe's Pizza, Keste, Motorino, and Rubirosa, all in Manhattan.

Box for Joe's on Carmine.

"A box that's not generic automatically gets more than one point," she explains. "Other points can be given for an original design or simply beautiful design, or having reheating instructions on the box."

Five-star boxes include Flatbread Company in Somerville, Massachusetts (for its sixties-psychedelic-looking box); Eataly (which deconstructs a classic pizza napoletana on its box); and Eddie's Pizza Truck. She singles out Eddie's as an example of "efficient" packaging—a shallow design for its super-thin pie.

All this is harder work than it sounds. If Chow orders a slice somewhere, she surely can't ask for a box to put it in, so she relies on the kindness of pizza countermen who hold up the box so she can photograph it.

"Sometimes I'll call a place beforehand and say, 'I have a really strange question—what does your pizza box look like?' They'll go get the box, describe it to me."

The strangest pizza box she's ever seen? A triangular one from Pizza Pizza in Bangkok featuring a long-legged Thai woman in an abbreviated French maid's outfit holding a pizza peel over a black-olive-and-green-pepper-topped pizza.

Pizza Pizza box, Bangkok.

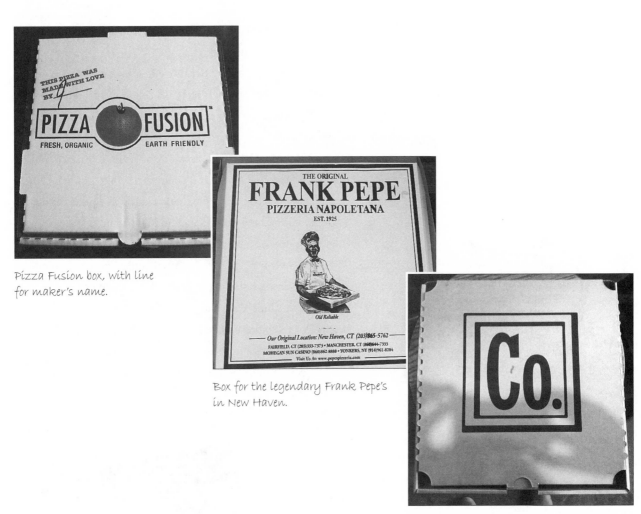

Pizza Fusion box, with line for maker's name.

Box for the legendary Frank Pepe's in New Haven.

The Co. box is a model of simplicity.

On its box, Pizzicato Gourmet Pizza in Encinitas, California, offers detailed instructions for cooking the "half-baked" pizza customers should order if they don't intend to eat it right away.

Pizza Fusion (New Jersey, Colorado, and elsewhere) has a space on the box where the pizza maker can sign his or her name.

The box from Frank Pepe in New Haven is in old-school black and white. Trattoria Cinque in Tribeca goes minimalist, and then some—a tiny label with the pizzeria's name, the rest an all-white box.

"It's good to see extra vents for better prevention of oversteaming," Chow says. "Conversely, some boxes may get points deducted for avoiding vents altogether."

Shirley Chow taking yet another pizza box home.

She calls the GreenBox for pizza, made of recycled cardboard and available in select pizzerias, "a great innovation in pizza box design." It's "eco-friendly and also functional—the top of the GreenBox breaks apart so that that it can be used as plates, while the bottom of the box can be transformed into a smaller container for any leftover slices."

Her least favorite boxes are those with nonpizzeria advertising.

"There'll be ads for Chase Bank or Target. That's no fun. It's just a billboard."

The French maid pizza box from Thailand is in her bedroom, and she talks about getting rid of it one day. So how was the pizza at Pizza Pizza?

"Really doughy," she replies.

So the box was better than the pizza?

"Oh yeah," she says with a laugh.

The World's Greatest Pizza Comedian

The guy with the unkempt but somehow stylish black hair—think mod cut meets gale-force winds—says he's proud of all the "J-level" celebrities he's managed to bring to his pizzeria at the corner of Mott and Kenmare.

So, Greg Barris, how would you describe what you do at L'asso?

"Eating," he says, laughing. "We're always working on new desserts, so I'm checking those out."

What is he trying to be, funny?

It comes easy to the city's only pizzeria owner/stand-up comedian. Barris has been a comedian since the tender age of fourteen. Pizza entrepreneur? That's come more recently, and by accident. He was walking home with a case of beer from every performer's nightmare—an empty house—when he stopped at L'asso one night.

Greg Barris outside
L'asso, which he co-owns.

102

The stand-up comic had been doing five shows a week at a theater space on Bond Street. The opening week was not exactly auspicious.

"The first one, twenty people came to," Barris recalls. "The second one, nobody came to."

A flop on one stage turned out to be a hit on another. Barris clicked with L'asso owner Rob Benevenga and started working as a waiter. And bartender. And occasional dealer for poker games in the basement. At the time, L'asso was open just for dinner and served only pizza. Benevenga had gone through five managers; Barris said, why not give me a chance?

Barris added lunch and brunch, started marketing and publicizing the restaurant, and, in the ultimate leap of faith, bought into the company.

In 2009, a panel from the 5-Boro Pizza Tour named L'asso Manhattan's best pizza. The stand-up comedian is too modest, at least publicly, to take credit for the honor, but he certainly played a key role in the pizzeria's rebirth.

Although he engineered L'asso's move to a more health-conscious, expansive menu (organic cheese and sauce, unbromated flour, a dozen new pizzas), he's focused on more pressing issues this Saturday afternoon. Like making sure "Heart of Darkness"—his monthly comic showcase, billed as "the World's Most Important Live Event"—goes off without a hitch. HOD shuttles between New York City, Los Angeles, San Francisco, and Florida, which makes for a schedule already complicated by such matters as making sure those desserts (try the salted caramel budino or pudding) are just right.

But comedy comes first—will always come first—in Barris's life story, even if his grandfather George Bekas ran the only restaurant ever located on the elevated tracks, the B&E Diner in Coney Island. Born in Brooklyn, Barris grew up in Winter Haven, Florida, which he is quick to mention is "the water skiing capital of the world." He worked at the famed Cypress Gardens park, with its lush gardens and water-skiing beauties.

"I would announce the ski shows. They made me do everything, paid me 25 cents above minimum wage. I worked my ass off."

Sidewalk message board, L'asso, Manhattan.

He longed for a different stage. At age fourteen, he performed at the Sak Comedy Lab, a two-hundred-seat improv theater in Orlando. At the time, he thought it was "the greatest thing ever. I was a little younger than everyone else, but it really didn't dawn on me."

The beer and wine board inside L'asso.

Despite a scholarship, he dropped out of the University of Central Florida to pursue a comedic career.

"I knew I wanted to do stand-up, I wanted to move to New York," he says. "I sold my car, sold everything, and moved in with my grandmother [Dimitra Beckas] in Bensonhurst."

With a laminated *Streetwise NYC* map in hand, he visited every comedy club in the city, dropping off tapes and a résumé. Only one club called him back—the Ha!

"The worst club, easily," he says with some affection. "Bad comedy."

He would hand out flyers on the sidewalk outside Ha!, then get to perform for five minutes onstage. He did it for eight months, earning about $150 a week.

Then he landed a job at Caroline's, another mix of grunt and glamour work—answering the phone, performing once or twice a week. One day he and a colleague pulled a practical joke. Caroline's phone number was nearly identical to an airline flight information number. When a man called to ask about his daughter's flight, Barris and his pal told him there seemed to be a problem with it. Caroline's manager got wind of the stunt and fired them both.

That's where the theater space on Bond Street and the case of beer come in. And his rebirth as pizza mogul. Barris calls L'asso "a very neighborhood casual salon-style table-service restaurant." He and Benevenga wanted to open a pizzeria in Los Angeles, but it fell through. They made up for it by opening L'asso EV (for East Village) in late 2011, and hope to open several more locations in the city.

The funny man is more than a mere dessert taster at L'asso; the dough here is his recipe, while the sauce comes from Benevenga's mom, whose garden supplies vegetables in the summer. Barris added pizzas to the menu, including a deep-dish, a brave move in a city where deep-dish is avoided if not scorned.

"There wasn't any deep-dish in New York; there was Uno, one place in Queens," Barris says. He breaks into a smile. "I wanted to do a major throwdown. Make a deep-dish, say, 'Screw you, Chicago!'"

He enlisted five ex–New Yorkers living in Chicago to be his test panel, and today the deep-dish is one of L'asso's more popular pizzas.

Barris switches between pizza and art and comedy effortlessly. One moment, he'll tell you about the possible long-term effects of bromated flour (bromate is a level-B2 "probable human" carcinogen but is used by the overwhelming majority of pizzerias around the country), and the next, about an upcoming performance art installation— a five-minute piece that includes sensory deprivation and "arpeggio microtones" in a pop-up space in Manhattan.

"You'll come out thinking you've just had a mushroom trip," he says, grinning.

Art and pizza mix well at L'asso; each month, the walls feature the work of a different artist. The "Campbell's Tomato Spray" can on the drop-down gate outside is done by noted pop artist Mr. Brainwash. The only stand-up going on at the Nolita location is done by the waitresses at each table, but Barris is adding a stage and screen to the East Village L'asso.

"People love to hate on pizza; it's probably the most hated thing on the Internet," he says when talk turns to online reviews of pizzerias.

Slice once published an uncomplimentary review of L'asso, which brings a smile to Barris's face. "They're just pawns on my pizza checkerboard," he says.

His favorite slice joints include Stromboli (First Avenue and St. Marks Place), South Brooklyn (various locations), Rosario's (Lower East Side), and Joe's on Carmine. His all-time favorite New York pizza, though, is Di Fara's.

Barris is a major food geek—he can break down every pizza on the menu and calls his collection of 3,500 cookbooks "the largest private cookbook collection" anywhere— but his heart is in comedy. Is there money in being funny?

"There's more money in it than you think," he replies. "There are maybe two thousand stand-up comedians in New York. Maybe four hundred are making any money out of it. The rest are doing it for free or for drink tickets."

The stand-up comedian, who describes his routine as "pretty absurd storytelling," has appeared on the MTV show *Warren the Ape*, "a puppet reality show." Wait, he can do better than that—he has showcased for Leno in Hermosa Beach, which meant a four-and-a-half-minute spot that appeared on nbc.com for a month.

How does he prep for a show? He eats lightly, thinks about jokes he'll do, and works out—pull-ups, push-ups, treadmill work. And don't forget his secret weapon: a dose of royal jelly (queen bees live on this stuff), propolis (a resinlike material honeybees collect from tree buds or sap flows), and eleuthero root (an herbal sedative and immune system stimulant).

"It's like goop; it's like hours of buzz," he says.

When asked whether he would choose pizza or comedy as his desert-island career, the self-described "world's greatest pizza comedian" takes a microsecond to reply.

The stage, and not anywhere near an oven.

"Comedy is like golf," Barris says. "You can do it until you die."

John's of Elmhurst

"My parents, Italian; my husband, Greek," says the older of the two women behind the counter at John's Pizzeria in Elmhurst, Queens.

"We came to the United States in 1962. There was a pizzeria nearby. I was walking around and stopped by one day. I became friends [with the co-owner]. She showed me how to make pizza." Quick smile. "Of course I make better pizza than them."

There are a handful of female-owned pizzerias in New York City; John's is likely the only one run by a mother and daughter. Rose Bagali and her daughter Susan make quite a team, Rose more reserved, Susan more earthy, greeting customers by first name, joking with the schoolboys who stop by every afternoon. One, Patrick, pops in every day just to say hi; he often doesn't even order a slice.

"We were two times in the *Daily News*," Rose says proudly, pulling out newspaper clips. John Bagali, her husband, opened the pizzeria in 1965 on the next block over; it moved to its current location, a former drugstore, in 1976. The pizza was thin then and will be thin fifty years from now. Why not thicker?

Susan and Rose Bagali, owners of John's of Elmhurst, Queens.

"Because I don't like that," Rose says sternly. "It is too much like bread."

Only she and her daughter make the pizza. They make dough every day, sauce every other day.

John's is located on a stretch of Grand Avenue populated with minimarkets, Chinese restaurants, and a psychic with a bust of Nefertiti in the window. At John's, open every day except Monday, no bills over $20 are accepted, and there are no restrooms. A poster on the wall is titled "Proverbi Italiani." Among them: "Arithmetic is not an opinion." A sign in the window proclaims, "Best Sicilian in town."

One regular here today, Mary, mourns that she doesn't come as often as she once did because she now lives seven blocks away.

"I walked in the rain today, no less," she says. "They must be doing something right."

The *Daily News* named John's best thin-crust slice in Queens.

NEWS NYDailyNews.com   Tuesday, March 16, 2010

BEST THIN-CRUST SLICE
John's Pizzeria; *85-02 Grand Ave.; Elmhurst; (718) 457-7561*
Last year's Five Borough Pizza Tour participants bestowed the top honor to this simple, thin-crust cheese pizza out of the borough's plethora of pizza joints. A large pie costs $14 and a slice goes for $2.25.

The customers are wonderful but sometimes say the funniest things. "A lady called up to order a Sicilian [whole pizza]," Susan recalled. "She said, 'My family doesn't like corners; can you make one without corners?' Another said, 'Can you cut my pizza into six pieces? Eight pieces is too much.'"

One delivery guy wanted to be paid more in the winter because it was cold. Susan's reply: "Then we'll pay you less in the summer because it's too hot."

She's one of the few pizzeria owners with a Facebook page who takes it seriously. Regulars from old-timers in Queens to soldiers in Iraq go online to say how much they love—or miss—John's. Witness this exchange:

> Sandra Tobar: Love ya mama!!
> John's Pizzeria: What a gloomy day! :-(Have a slice of pizza to brighten your day. Just mention code "gloomy day" and get 25 cents off a slice.
> Sandra Tobar: Awesome!!!! The best pizza Ever!!!!
> John's Pizzeria: Just want to thank you guys for your loyalty. Mama says she loves you too. :-)
> Sandra Tobar: The funny [thing] is that John's Pizzeria is not only a place to eat, but a home away from home with a nice warm slice for dinner Thank you Mama and Susie for that!!! :) love ya ladies!
> Chris Ortiz: Love johns pizza!!!! Ayyyyy . . . OHHHHH
> Carlito's Way: Facebook need to make Smell a vision lol. . . . Best pizza ever.

So what's the secret to John's success? Not the cheese, not the sauce, but a piece of worn metal that maybe cost a quarter when new.

"No one does this," Rose says of the mesh screen on which the pizza rests. "It makes the bottom very clean. Other places, the bottom gets very dark and burnt. Not ours. It's our secret."

Two uniformed cops and one plainclothes detective stop in. "All my police boys are here," Rose says, smiling.

Sitting nearby is Robert Mitchell, a former deputy sheriff in New Orleans who went on disability after being hit by a drunk driver. He is separated from his wife; she and their son live in the Bronx. "I have him every other week," Mitchell says. "When I pick him up, the first thing he says is 'I want to go to John's.'"

Another group of schoolboys, this time from Brooklyn Tech, pile in. There is some good-natured taunting back and forth, and at least one serious moment.

"Every Monday," says Brian Larzuela, "we are sad."

The Greatest Thing Since . . .

Top story in pizza the past year?

Meredith Smith on *Slice* singled out square pies (whether Sicilian, Grandma, or Roman), fried pizza, and breakfast pizza.

Pizza Marketplace's top stories included the sizzling stock performance of the Big Three (Domino's, Papa John's, and Pizza Hut), online ordering, and deep discounts.

For me, it was easy, at least when it came to the New York pizza scene.

Dollar slices.

Pizza purists may cringe, but let's face it, there are probably a lot more people scarfing down dollar slices at this moment than forking over $20-plus for a gourmet pizza.

In the past year, dollar and 99-cent slices (it's only a matter of time for 98-cent and 97-cent slices, apparently) have sprung up faster than pop-up stores.

"Look, if you're eating dollar pizza, you're pretty much broke, drunk, or hungry and out of options. So flavor's not a huge deal," says Adam Kuban, founder of *Slice*.

I'll politely disagree; the slice joints that have proliferated in midtown Manhattan are packed with people—high school students, office workers, tourists, even suits—who not only look sober but don't appear in any danger of hitting the poverty level.

Mamani Pizza, Avenue A.

109

The 99¢ Fresh Pizza store outside the Port Authority bus terminal.

FDR 99¢ Pizza on East 2nd Street.

Dollar slices have been around longer than you may think; 99¢ Fresh Pizza opened in Hell's Kitchen in 2001. 99¢ Fresh Pizza has spawned similarly named knockoffs— 99¢ Slice Pizza and FDR 99¢ Slice Pizza.

Dollar slices are a Manhattan phenomenon, but word of advice (or warning) to the other boroughs: they're heading your way. As of this writing there are a handful of non-Manhattan dollar-slice places including Empire Slices in Bushwick and Brooklyn

Sign outside 2 Bros. on St. Marks Place.

Pizza on Fulton Street in Brooklyn, where the dollar slice is offered from 2 to 5 P.M. weekdays only. But when Papa John's starts offering dollar slices (as of now, at just four of its fifteen city locations), you know dollar slices are here to stay.

The two big players are 99¢ Fresh Pizza and 2 Bros. Pizza; *Slice* founder Adam Kuban calls them the Coke and Pepsi of the dollar-slice world. But other slice joints have carved out their own niches—and may be even better than the Big Two.

2 Bros. opened its first store, on St. Marks Place, in 2007. Eli Halali is one of two brothers who own the chain.

99¢ Fresh Pizza is owned by Abdul Mohammad, a Bangladeshi immigrant and former newsstand operator.

As of this writing, there are about fifty pizzerias offering dollar slices in New York if you count the multiple locations of 2 Bros. and 99¢ Fresh Pizza. The latter's stand at Ninth Avenue and West 41st Street boasts not only a great location—behind the Port Authority Bus Terminal—but also a low-rent charm, especially at night, when the harsh fluorescent lighting, chipped neon sign, and stark red lettering ("2 Slice & Can Soda or Water 2.75") create a perfect movie set for a pizza-themed thriller. Or something.

First rule of thumb when ordering at any dollar-slice joint: Don't expect to have a lengthy conversation with the counterman about global warming, the price of gas, or the Yankees. The object is to sell slices as fast as possible and keep the line moving.

99¢ Fresh Pizza's nine locations are situated in low-rent, high-traffic-volume areas.

"If I pay high $15,000 to $20,000 rent, I can't do dollar slices," Mohammad told the *New York Times*.

2 Bros., the other dollar-slice heavyweight, actually started as an afterthought. When the first outlet opened on St. Marks Place, the dollar-slice grand-opening special proved so popular the owners made it a permanent fixture.

Mohammed of 99¢ Fresh Pizza estimates he makes about 15 to 20 cents profit per slice. That may be an understatement. Tom Miner, a consulting principal at Technomic, a Chicago-based food industry consulting firm, told the *Wall Street Journal* that the wholesale price of a typical dollar slice is about 45 cents—25 to 30 cents for the cheese, 10 to 12 cents for the dough, 5 cents for the sauce.

No wonder delis and markets around the city are jumping on the dollar-slice bandwagon.

Kuban did a throwdown between dollar-slice heavyweights 99¢ Fresh Pizza and 2 Bros. His decision on *Slice*: "Overall, the 2 Bros. pizza had a better flavor than the 99¢ Fresh Pizza slice. While the 99FP slice was better balanced in terms of crust-sauce-cheese ratio, that's not necessarily a good thing here, since that balance allows you to taste the sauce. It's flavored heavily with what tastes like powdered garlic—acrid and almost metallic-tasting. When scraped away on its own, the 2 Bros. sauce is bland but at least does not assault your tongue."

The city's best dollar slice? Thought you'd never ask. I hit every dollar-slice joint in the city over two days; it was easily the cheapest part of the research for this book. And

FACT:
Each American
eats nearly
fifty slices a year.

Dollar-slice sign.

often the most painful. You get what you pay for, and the typical dollar slice skimps on size, cheese, sauce—and taste. But there are several commendable ones out there—in some unlikely locations.

My ranking of the city's top dollar slices:

1. Z Deli Pizzeria, Eighth Avenue
2. 2 Bros. Pizza, various locations
3. Gray's Papaya, Sixth Avenue
4. Mamani Pizza, Avenue A
5. Mike's Pizza, East 23rd Street

(Full reviews of dollar-slice pizzerias appear in the back of the book, alphabetical by borough.)

So what did I learn from my excursion to Dollar Slice World? For a dollar, you shouldn't expect much, and many slices sampled were tasteless at best and borderline-inedible at worst. The above five stood out. None are great slices, but for a buck they're great bargains.

"Although the $2.50 slice might be of slightly better quality—most people don't

The Papa John's on West 28th Street is one of four Papa John's in the city to offer dollar slices.

care," says Jason Feirman of the *I Dream of Pizza* blog. "If you're a homeless person on the corner of 43rd Street, or a drunk NYU student on St. Marks Place, you could care less. People will always be looking for deals in New York City. And with the competitive nature of the city, someone will always be trying to offer you a product at a cheaper price."

My take: If slices can be offered for a dollar, they certainly can be offered for 85, even 75, cents. And that is a development that will have pizza fiends shuddering with delight—or dread.

The Pizza Net

For the latest developments in the pizza universe, nothing beats a pizza blog. Breathlessly awaiting the verdict on that new pizzeria in Manhattan or Brooklyn? Chances are someone will post a review within hours of its opening. Heading to Rochester or Columbus or Portland and want to know the best slice places? There's a blog out there for you.

How many pizza blogs are there? Who knows—they pop up faster than quick-rising yeast. What is known is that there are close to 200 million blogs worldwide (and 550 million websites).

Here's a collection of some favorite pizza blogs. Not all are New York–centric, but all are informative, funny, generally dripping with flavor and loaded with attitude.

New York-centric

Me Myself & Pie. There are several Me Myself & Pies out there. One is a blog run by a woman who spent a year cooking her way through her favorite *Cooking Light* recipes. Another is a Facebook page maintained by a pie maker in Austin. And then there is the Pizza Commander, Brooks Jones, who is working on a feature-length documentary "about this divine cuisine." He gets around—there are review of pizzerias not just in New York but Boston, Chicago, Charleston, San Francisco, Cancun, and elsewhere.

Sample entry:

> To be quite honest I like my sausage in large chunks as opposed to sliced, cubed, crumbled, or any other B.S., but this didn't seem to fall into any of these categories. The texture wasn't amazing, but the flavor was. You can see some fennel mixed up in there if you look closely. This pizza was officially awesome.

▶ *pizzacommander.blogspot.com*

FACT: Americans eat 100 acres of pizza every day— about 350 slices per second.

Morta di Fame. "My name is Jen; I'm half crazy and love to cook," says Jen Galatioto, founder of *Morta di Fame*, which means "dying of hunger" in Italian. It's more about food in general, but there are reports of trips to New Park Pizza, Paulie Gee's, and elsewhere.

Sample entry:

> I was looking forward to her mother Aurora's famous sweet and sour meatballs, which were amazing. I wanted to know the recipe but with Sicilians there are no written-down recipes. You just kind of ask and take what you can get. There was a lot of her mother telling me the recipe in Sicilian and Fra translating, going, "How do you say that?" to me. Uh? I don't know. And I am like, Rocco, "what is she saying?" Then Rocco just repeats the word in Sicilian multiple times waving his hands, as if hearing it 10 times in Sicilian will somehow make me understand it in English.

▶ *mortadifame.blogspot.com*

New York Pizza Project. "We're hitting pizzerias throughout the five boroughs to capture the distinctive people and places behind New York's quintessential food," say the team members—Corey, Gabe, Ian, Nick, and Tim. The goal is to hit a hundred slice joints throughout the city.

Better-than-average photos. More of an oral history of NYC pizza than reviews, and compelling.

Sample entry:

> "I been in here since I was 10 yrs old with my mother and father. I'm not a Joe that just started after I lost my job on Wall Street and said, 'What am I gonna do? I'll open up a pizzeria.' That's a lot of what's goin' on today."

▶ *nypizzaproject.com.*

Pizza Rules! Occasional pizza blog by designer/skateboarder/musician Nick Sherman, formerly of Boston, now of Brooklyn. It's one of the most eye-catching blogs out there, with a red-and-white-checked background and a heady mix of reviews, music video, and pizza odds and ends. Nick spent an entire month—April 2010—eating nothing but pizza. The first three things he ate when it was over: a single sunflower seed, a slice of cold leftover pizza, and a sandwich with cherry tomatoes, fresh mozzarella, and olive oil.

Sample entry:

> I do have some gripes though. First of all, our marinara pie had a huge scorch mark that went straight through (see photo below). I'm all for the typical charring of any pizza that is cooked in a really hot oven like this one, and

actually prefer a little spotting; but this was a huge solid chunk of pure carbon that, instead of accenting the flavor, made that slice basically like biting in to a solid piece of carbon.

► *pizzarules.com*

Slice. The city's—and nation's—foremost pizza blog, packed with reviews, trends, and breaking pizza news. One feature is "The Daily Slice," which highlights a slice from somewhere in the United States. Adam Kuban, who started the blog in 2003, sold it to seriouseats.com in 2006 but still contributes. It's the go-to place for pizza obsessives everywhere.

Sample entry:

> Recently, I found myself in Providence with an empty stomach and an hour to spare on a sunny Saturday afternoon, so naturally I decided to see what I could find in the way of a good slice. I made my way up and over College Hill to Thayer Street, the main shopping-and-eating-drag on the far side of RISD and Brown, to check out Nice Slice Pizzeria.
>
> Nice Slice is a hipster-slash-hippie slice joint, with RISD alum Shepard Fairey's Andre the Giant posters plastered on its walls and a substantial portion of their menu friendly to a vegan clientele.

► *slice.seriouseats.com*

Slice Harvester. Colin Hagendorf, a waiter at a Brooklyn diner and former puppeteer, spent two and a half years hitting every slice joint in Manhattan, 362 in all. He originally wanted to hit all 1,600 pizzerias in the city, but he found that was a bit much. More attitude than most, with a side order of expletives.

Sample entry:

> And much like the ambiance of P & P Delight, the flavor of this pizza was nearly nonexistent. Matt called it "Ghost Pizza." Something about this whole place reminded me of that haunted train in Final Fantasy III, but sadly, that reference is probably lost on a bulk of my readership. Anyway, this pizza tasted like a piece of winterfresh that you've chewed all the flavor out of. You know how there's still like, a taste to old gum, but it tasted like NOTHING? This pizza is like that. And the texture was a nightmare. Matt said, "you don't even need your teeth to bite this pizza!" and Chuck was like, "yeah, it's like eating a piece of cake." I thought the crust sucked, but Matt seemed to find it inoffensive, at least, so there's that.

► *sliceharvester.blogspot.com*

"There's a pizza place near where I live that sells only slices. In the back, you can see a guy tossing a triangle in the air."
—comedian
Steven Wright

31 Days of Pizza. Sean Taylor celebrates National Pizza Month (October, but you knew that) by eating a slice every day of the month at a different pizzeria. In 2011, he completed part of his mission in New York City, the rest in Italy, on vacation (Day 22 was a slice inside JFK Airport). There's little on the pizza consumed, but you'll enjoy the journey.

Sample entry:

> This pizza meal marks only the second time my mom has met my fiancée's parents. The first time was a passover seder so, obviously, this one involved a lot more carbs and a lot less gefilte fish.

▶ *31daysofpizza.com*

Elsewhere

Baltimore Pizza Club. "Our goal is to promote the thoughtful consumption of [the] greatest food on Earth," according to the club's mission statement. "We strive to help you, the pizza consumer, make well-informed decisions in all places that your life intersects with pizza. We truly love pizza from a deep place in our bodies." Members include Alicia, Max, Emily "Slaughter," Jordan, Sara Seidman, and Richie Millions.

Sample entry:

> The crust overall was very good. It was doughy, yet crunchy at the same time. All the ingredients were fresh and Egyptian pizza deserves props for some innovative flavor combinations. That said, all they needed to do was push those a little bit further to fulfill their promises of exotic pizza delight. The fundamentals are solid, but the falafel pizza of our dreams remains just out of reach.

▶ *baltimorepizzaclub.blogspot.com*

Best Pizza in Hong Kong. Posts from a "gal" named Duffy living in Hong Kong and her search for good pizza, which she considers "the most delicious food in the world hands down." Great pizza? From her posts, it sounds like it's a challenge to find even average pizza in HK. She rates crust, sauce, toppings, and ambiance on a scale of 1 to 10 (in a review of frozen pizza bought at the Great supermarket, Admiralty, she doesn't rate the ambiance because "I was in my pajamas in my apartment").

Sample entry:

Sicilian slice,
House of Pizza &
Calzone, Brooklyn.

Plain slice,
House of Pizza
& Calzone,
Brooklyn.

Biggie Smalls mural next to Not Ray's, Brooklyn.

Murals next to Pizza on the Run, Coney Island.

Warning sign,
Arome Deli & Pizza,
Manhattan

Chained pizza maker,
Famous Ben's,
Manhattan.

Bleecker Street Pizza, Manhattan.

Grandpa's Brick Oven Pizza, Manhattan.

The best Christmas decorations at any NYC pizzeria, Grandpa's, Manhattan.

Sajid Alam, owner,
Hell's Kitchen
Pizza, Manhattan.

The city's biggest pizza slice.
Koronet Pizza, Manhattan.

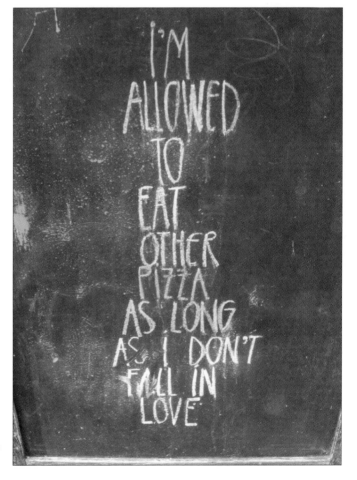

I'M ALLOWED TO EAT OTHER PIZZA AS LONG AS I DON'T FALL IN LOVE

Sign outside Lil' Frankie's,
Manhattan.

Another day on the job, Manhattan.

Sam's Famous Pizza, Harlem.

Mural, South Brooklyn Pizza,
Manhattan.

Dollar-slice joint,
Manhattan.

Pizza Suprema,
Eighth Avenue,
Manhattan.

La Villa Pizzeria, Howard Beach.

Street scene, Rosario's Deli, Queens.

Rosa's Pizza, Queens.

Mural, Nucci's South Italian Restaurant & Pizzeria, Staten Island.

City's most colorful
pizzeria menu.
Salvatore of Soho,
Staten Island.

My pizza sampling was done wherever, whenever. Staten Island.

You eat where you can.

1. I don't love the sauce. Please see me after class for more details.

2. I am just as crazy about giant pizza slices as the next gal, but the size of these slices is unambiguously, positively, categorically and outrageously ridiculous, some might even say preposterous, and almost as unnecessarily absurd as this completely excessive string of words describing the size.

3. Seriously though, I asked them to cut them in half the second time. This isn't a too much of a good thing is a bad thing situation, it's just impossible to eat. Especially if you eat it standing in the street outside the store—as God intended for you to eat it.

► *bestpizzainhongkong.blogspot.com*

FACT:
Beijing and Shanghai have about seven hundred pizzerias each.

Chicago Pizza Club. Chi-town is no second city when it comes to pizza, according to the members of the Chicago Pizza Club, who include Adam, Andrew, Neil, Jennifer, Rebecca, Mikel, Amanda, Kelly, and Francisco, "El Presidente." Photos could be better, but good straightforward reviews.

Sample entry:

> This pie has great finesse. Like an undersized defensive tackle, it does not overwhelm with mass, but wins with technique and elusiveness. For instance, the onions were substantial, but melted away in my mouth. The pepperoni gave the pie porky protein, but did not overwhelm. The pie was deep, but the crust was light. The amalgam of cheese, sauce, and toppings flowed, but maintained individual structural integrity. Some would call this pie, "stuffed light." For many, including this [reviewer], that is just fine.

► *chicagopizzaclub.com*

Diary of a Pizza Girl. How many female pizza delivery persons are out there? Can't be many, and none can tell a story quite like the Pizza Girl. She started delivering in Austin in October 2008; the blog chronicles her delivery adventures and misadventures, loved and hated customers and colleagues, reviews, and pretty much life in general. It's by turns funny and frightening. An absolute must-read.

Sample entry:

> Last night was the first time I ever got my pepper spray ready to use. It was 8:30, I was delivering to a trailer park where the house numbers are impossible to see. I finally spot the house and there's a couple of guys standing outside. One of them runs up the walkway to get his "aunt" who's going to pay. I walk up to stand on the porch as she comes out and the second guy starts following

me up the walk. I felt penned in, so I reached into my pocket and pulled my keys out. I put them in my pizza-holding hand, so that the bag concealed them and I was completely ready to throw the pizza at one guy while I pushed the other down the stairs, using the pepper spray if necessary. Luckily nothing like that happened, but it kind of freaked me out anyway.

▶ *apizzagirl.blogspot.com*

LA Pizza. The founder promises to eat at a different slice joint around L.A. at least five days a week, although it appears he's slacked off a little. Reviews of places like Garage Pizza, Golden Mean Vegan Cafe, Hard Times Pizza, Mother Dough, and Pinball Pizza.

Sample entry:

The pizza had cheese spots. Instead of shredded cheese, it was slices, small slices of mozzarella. There are of course many other places that cook their Margherita Pizza like this, but they aren't cut in such small sizes. I don't like too much cheese, but I was worried about this one because I thought there might not be enough. Surprisingly, there was just the right amount. Whether it was fresh or not was hard to tell, the cheese flavor wasn't that prominent, seeing as it wasn't covering the whole pizza.

▶ *losangelespizza.blogspot.com*

Liza and Gary's DC Pizza Blog. "Self-proclaimed pizza experts" scout out the best pizza in the nation's capital. Straightforward but detailed reviews, minimum of photos. Liza and Gary each rate the pizzerias on a scale of 1 ("abysmal") to 4 ("top notch!").

Sample entry:

The hostess got us a high chair for Molly. OK, can I go on a side rant here? When we got the high chair, the clasp on the strap was broken. I swear, 90% of the time we use a restaurant high chair, the clasp is broken. Do people not understand how to snap these things? Is there some major design flaw there? Or is some rogue child hater going restaurant to restaurant, systematically destroying high chairs so as to never again to have to listen to a screaming toddler while trying to enjoy a meal? Graffiato was open for like, a MONTH at this point, and the strap is already broken. What's up with that?
   All right, back to the blog.

▶ *dcpizzablog.blogspot.com*

New York Pizza Finder. Intriguing—not a guide to New York pizza but one to New York pizza elsewhere. Like Decatur, Georgia. Or Dallas. Or Honolulu. Founder T. Sliker, a

Jersey native now living in the South, rates pizza according to the Sliker Rating Scale—40 percent of the score is based on whether it's thin-crust, 10 percent on whether pizza is available by the slice, 10 percent on whether the slices are large, 10 percent on whether the place is "run by Italians," and so on.

Sample entry:

> I crossed several lanes of traffic and did a U-Turn and walked up the steps to a pleasant surprise—La Pizza Mia Pizzeria. I ordered the lunch special, 2 slices and a coke for under $5. It was delicious. The place was run by two Italian women who spoke Italian to one another.
>
> The slices were perfect! Just what I wanted. I didn't do the math, but I'm pretty sure this place ranked 95 on the Sliker Scale (no Sicilian that I saw).

▶ *newyorkpizzafinder.com*

The Pizza Files. Former pizza delivery boy and pizzeria assistant manager on a search for the best pizza in St. Louis, where he lives. For his twelfth wedding anniversary, he took his wife out for pizza—actually, it was her idea. Reviews are simple, and he needs a copy editor (the "it's" instead of "its" will drive you nuts), but it's an informative guide to pizza in the heartland.

Sample entry:

> In the future I would probably order the Margherita over The Good Pie, as I suspect it was the cheese adding the extra wetness. Although the Funghi needed to be folded up it didn't appear to have the same wetness going on as The Good Pie. The Funghi with it's extra cheese and roasted mushrooms was [a] very different experience and also very good.

▶ *pizzafiles.com*

Pizza Goon. "The best of the pizza blogs," John Gutekanst modestly says of *Pizza Goon*. It's different, anyway, written from the perspective of a pizza maker; Gutekanst owns Avalanche Pizza in Athens, Ohio. He's more interested in baking and finding quality, sometimes unusual, ingredients for pizza and bread. Rabbit pizza, anyone? Lots of recipes. Tech-laden, but highly informative.

Sample entry:

> I use a cold-maturation for my pre-ferments. This enables the yeasts to activate slower and I think, because I am using old grains like spelt, coaxes more flavor out of the whole grains. Thus, when I plan to bake (which is every day), I start by feeding spelt and high-protein flours to my pre-ferment that

was made with the natural mother (10 percent starter to 90 percent high gluten flour spelt and water). Then I feed twice a day for a week with the dough near the pizza ovens (60–75 degrees). I throw out or recycle 80 percent of the preferment and add another 80 percent flour and water, mixing with my hands. At this temp, the yeast is in [its] perfect environment to eat, eat, eat, then turn to an almost lifeless soup. After the week, I mix one more time and retard the pre ferment in my walk-in for a much needed rest for a few days.

▶ *pizzagoon.com*

Pizzalicious. Lauren Vincelli's blog focuses on pizza in Richmond, Virginia. Her favorite pizzeria there: 8½, which also happens to be her "all-time favorite" movie. A mix of reviews and video, plus items on pizza-related equipment and apparel.

Sample entry:

Yesterday my friend Kenny shared a cute recipe with me that his grandpappy shared with him. He called it Pappy's Poor Man Pizza. We made a vegan version because, well, Kenny is vegan. It was DELICIOUS! Pizza is for everyone! We used Diya brand vegan cheese and it is great for pizzas! You even get the ninja turtle cheese stretch. Bonus!

▶ *pizzaliciousblog.blogspot.com*

Pizza Ottawa. Because you never know when you'll find yourself in the Canadian capital. Jim and Mike are your guides to places like Super Duper Pizza, House of Pizza Walkley, and Tennessy Willems. Straightforward reviews—nothing but the facts—and no photos, but they provide an insight into what passes for pizza over the border.

Sample entry:

As the pizza is cooked in a wood-fired oven, the strength of this pizza is the crust. The crust is thin, with a delicious woody flavour. It is crispy and chewy in all the right spots, and the charred bits and the edge of the crust (where it's airy and bubbly) are the best. The flavour is light, reminiscent of matzoh (water and flour) but with much more depth.

▶ *blindstare.com/pizza*

Pizza Slayer. "A pizza publication/blog centered in the Central Ohio region" that welcomes "local recommendations and stuff." The dialogue is right out of central pizza casting—"We totally went to Plaza Pizza but they are closed on Sunday" and "Two older dudes gave this place a nice feel" are typical observations. Funny, informative, kind of a stoner's guide to pizza.

"The perfect lover is one who turns into a pizza at 4 A.M."
—Charles Pierce

Sample entry:

> In a hipster neighborhood. You walk upstairs and it's like a nice-looking, well lit diner, kind of. Photo machine, indie rock jukebox, neon lights and a bum sleepsitting on a corner stool. I got an awesome T-Shirt for only 5 bucks, after we ate, naturally.

▶ *14inchesoflove.blogspot.com*

Pizza Snobo. "We review the best pizza pies, pizzerias, delivery pizza, and pizza by the slice. Whether it's pizza in New York City, Paris, or Hawaii, *Pizza Snobo* tells it like it is." One twist: All pizzas are rated 1 to 8; 1 is "worst," 2 "pretty bad," 5 "very good," 7 "fantastic," 8 "out of this world." Only four pizzerias had received a 7 or 8 grade as of this writing: Rubirosa, Motorino, Artichoke Basille, and Keste, all in Manhattan. To-the-point reviews; no fawning over the cornicione and whether there was enough fleur de sel on top.

Sample entry:

> Slices are $3 plus tax. The cheese is probably the best part, with a decent blend that is a notch above your typical pizzeria. The cheese-to-sauce ratio was good, but the sauce's flavor tended toward the bland side. The crust, which is the draw in the first place, turned out to be greasy and not very memorable. Get a slice with a topping, because it will help disguise the merely average base pie.

▶ *pizzasnobo.com*

The Rochester NY Pizza Blog. One of the better regional pizza blogs, this blog posts reviews on a regular basis, unlike the erratic, irregular pace of others. One helpful part: You can go straight to the pizzerias graded A, B+, B, and so on.

Sample entry:

> As for that crust—visually, it bore all the hallmarks of a great, crisp crust from a super-hot oven, with charring along the edge and underneath. In fact, in some spots on the bottom, the outer surface of the crust was charred right through (see bottom photo). And it did have a certain smokiness to it.
>
> So it was a surprise to find that the crust was really quite soft. It wasn't mushy or spongy or anything like that, it was just not at all crisp.

▶ *rochesternypizza.blogspot.com*

Sex and Pizza. "Diary of a single, almost 30 year-old, queer, college graduated, pizza delivery girl and phone sex operator." What more needs to be said? A log of hours worked (as pizza delivery girl, that is), deliveries completed, and tips made, with general observations on life.

Sample entry:

> worked three and a half hours, took six deliveries, got $9 reimbursement, and made $26.30 in tips (thank you $8 tip guy) equalling $5.88 per delivery and $16.71 an hour after taxes.
>
> now it's Friday night, and I'm home watching a movie because nobody I know wants to go out. everyone has gotten old and boring. hmph.

▶ *sexandpizza.wordpress.com*

Syracuse NY Pizza Blog. Rochester has a pizza blog, why not Syracuse? "The reality of the Syracuse area is that while pizza is very easy to find, really GOOD pizza is hard to find," says the Pizza Geek, the blog's founder. "We need more pizza research in Central New York!" The Geek is more opinionated, edgier than most, even if the photos could be displayed much better.

Sample entry:

> The Artisan does not have the oil-salt-garlic-spice topping added to the rim. I'm not exaggerating when I say this, but the crust was roughly equivalent to a bargain frozen pizza crust. The word "cardboard" truly came to mind. And to be clear, DRY cardboard. There was no chewiness, no complex flavor, just a dry biscuit or cracker-like taste and small crumb texture. It is just about the worst crust I've ever had.

▶ *pizzageek.wordpress.com*

This Is Pizza. "Seeking out the best pies in America, one pizzeria at a time." Well, the best pies in Seattle and Portland, anyway. Adam Lindsley describes himself as a "voracious pizza fanatic." Better written than most.

Sample entry:

> Thankfully, Hotlips does sell individual slices, and I think that's the way to go here. Even their small pizzas are grossly overpriced (they start at $15.50 and just go up and up from there). None of the ingredients are particularly noteworthy, so what is it you're paying for? According to the Hotlips website, it's sustainability and community. Commendable, to be sure, but I only have so much cash budgeted for eating out, and sustainability and community aren't enough to get me to open my wallet for them again.

▶ *thisispizza.blogspot.com*

General Sites

Cheese Reporter. Informative, exhaustive, and weirdly compelling. The latest news and trends from the cheese world—"Allied Blending Introduces Pathogen Inhibitor Technology to Enhance Safety of Shredded Cheese," "Tetra Pak Launches Next Generation of Tetra Tebel Cheddar Blockformers," and so on. The same issue that tells us "Global dairy consumption expected to grow 58% by 2050" reports "Feed given to dairy cows blamed for high levels of cancer-causing toxin found in milk in China." There's more where that came from.

▶ *cheesereporter.com*

In Search of the Perfect Pie. Ryan Sanders's pizza-making blog is one of the better ones of its kind, full of recipes, tips, and videos of the likes of Tony Gemignani and Peter Reinhart.

Sample entry:

> When the pizza came out, it looked as if it had not risen at all—I suspect that my long rest in the fridge negated any effect the baking powder had, and the double acting feature was all but absent. The dough baked very thin, but because of the high oil content, it was very crispy—it began to taste like a homemade cracker after a few bites. There was good snap, it supported the weight of the toppings, it had a real buttery flavor (even though there was no actual butter in the dough)—all in all, it wasn't bad.

▶ *insearchoftheperfectpie.com*

FACT: About 5 billion pizzas are sold around the world every year.

International Pizza Expo. The latest on the industry's biggest annual event. Six thousand pizza operators, nearly five hundred exhibitors, seventy-five seminars, World Pizza Games dough-spinning finals, an international pizza-baking contest, and much more.

▶ *pizzaexpo.com*

International Pizza Punk Day. This "global holiday that will replace Christmas" started in London twelve years ago. Sounds like fun; it encourages supporters to acquaint themselves with vegan pizza making, throw potluck pizza parties (you make the pizza, friends bring ingredients), and "gather copious amounts of alcohol—or grape juice for the straight-edgers—and old punk tapes or CDs." International Pizza Punk Day, in case you didn't know already, is December 26.

▶ *eroding.org.uk/pizzapunx.htm*

Legends of Pizza Blog. "Pizza promoter" Albert Grande wants to honor "the pizzaiolo, who put their heart and soul into each pizza they make." Interviews with various pizza personalities, plus pizza industry news. Grande also maintains the pizzatherapy.com site.

► *legendsofpizza.com*

Passion 4 Pizza. Run by "a beautiful Italian-American girl from Long Island" who met "a nice Jewish boy from Brooklyn" and fell in love. She is Lillian d'Eustachio, he is Cary Steiner, and their blog is a pleasant hodgepodge of news, reviews, and their adventures in pizza making.

Sample entry:

> *Patsy's is historic New York coal-fired pizza. We've gotten used to tasting fresh mozz on the pizza that comes from glowing coals, but Patsy's regular pie is so delicious we didn't mind at all. For our tastes, the added basil enhanced the overall flavor, but both halves [of] our pie were excellent: just the right char, perfect balance of dough, cheese and sauce—everything you look for in great pizza. The crust, which to us is the most important part, was light with lots of airy holes in the* cornicione, *the outer crust. It had snap, a certain crispness without being crunchy. For us, it could have been a little chewier, but who's complaining?*

► *passion-4-pizza.com*

Pizza.com. The ultimate pizza URL. DDC, a domain development company, bought the name for $2.6 million in 2008 and hopes to turn pizza.com into the leading online pizza resource. Right now, you can type in a zip code or your address and find all the pizzerias nearby—the Silver Bow Pizza Parlor in Butte, Montana, for example, or Magoo's Pizza Waikiki in Honolulu. Lots of fun pizza videos and games, too.

► *pizza.com*

Pizza Delivery Stories. "True stories in the life of a part-time pizza delivery driver." The founder is Kevin L., a divorced dad with "a mountain of debt" who remarried and got a second job as pizza delivery man to augment his income. His pizza delivering has slowed because he's busy with dad and other duties, but he promises more stories in the future.

Sample entry (it's long, but it's a great Tolstoyan pizza story, so it's quoted in its entirety):

The Journey of a Quarter

> This is actually 2 stories, that both happened on the same night and both involved the same US Quarter. I'm pretty sure this happened in the fall of 2005 but I'm not positive. I know it was a chilly and rainy night.

I had a delivery to a public housing facility. I had no expectations of getting a tip. The order was for 2 medium pizzas (with coupon) for $14.98. Add in the $1.25 delivery charge and the total was $16.23.

I arrive at the building, get buzzed in, ride up the slower-than-molasses elevator, and knock on the door with their food. The customer answers the door with $16. I quote the price and the customer yells back into their apartment, "Hey do you have a quarter?"

What I hear in response makes me cringe. "I think there's one on the bathroom floor."

The customer disappears around the corner, and reappears with a 25-cent piece, saying "Yeah, there was." I pocket the money, trying not to touch the coin, give them their food, and proceed with my night.

Sometime around midnight I get a delivery to the far end of our delivery zone. This time the total is something like $20.74. Could have been 2 large pizzas and an extra cup of garlic sauce, I'm not exactly sure.

What I do know is that as I was standing at the door in the cold rain, a man in his early 20s handed me a $20 bill and then, like the customer before, called back into the house, "Mom, do you have a dollar?"

There was no immediate answer, but the guy didn't move to go find his mother, instead he just stood there and yelled out a few more times.

Meanwhile I am getting wetter and wetter. I realize I am not getting a tip from this guy, and I owe him back a quarter. Hmmmm . . . . .

I reach into my pocket and there it is, the quarter from the bathroom floor. I pull it out and get it ready to give this guy. Finally he goes into another room and returns with his dollar. I hand him the food and hold out the quarter.

"Keep it," he says.

"No, I really couldn't," I reply.

He still doesn't hold out his hand, so I flip the coin into the air, like the referee at the start of a football game. It lands with a jingle near his [feet] as I turn and head for my car.

"Hey, you don't have to throw it at me," he calls out after me.

As soon as I got moving I got out my cell phone and call back to the store to warn our manager. "Ward, if a customer calls and says that I threw a quarter at him, here's what really happened . . ." and I describe the events that just transpired.

Sure enough, before Ward hung up with me, I heard someone in the background say, "Ward, manager call, line 2."

Ward handled it well, and was very supportive. He asked the guy if it was his money, and when the guy said he should come up and beat the driver (me) up, Ward asked if he was making a threat, as Ward would be happy to call the police if he was. That pretty much ended the discussion.

And that ends the story of the journey of the quarter. From bathroom floor, to my pocket, back to non-tipping customer.

▶ *pizzadeliverystories.blogspot.com*

Pizza Making. Every possible pizza-making question, concern, problem, and issue is addressed in the forums here. "Help!" pleaded Dave, a user. "I need emergency focaccia for tonight!" Online help appeared immediately. Separate sections on New York, Chicago, Neapolitan, American, cracker, thick, California, Sicilian, and focaccia styles of pizza, plus gluten-free, specialty grain, dessert pizzas—and more.

▶ *pizzamaking.com*

Pizza Marketplace. Go-to source for the latest pizza business news and developments, not to mention "deep industry insights." There are reports and Q&As about food safety, health and nutrition, risk management, signage, sauce, toppings, et cetera.

▶ *pizzamarketplace.com*

Pizza Wikipedia. You knew this was coming. Wish there were more content; the "Pizza Around the World" section breaks down pizza in just eleven countries. In São Paolo, 1.4 million pizzas are consumed daily.

▶ *en.wikipedia.org/wiki/pizza*

United States Pizza Team. What, you didn't know there was an official U.S. Pizza Team? They're pizza makers and "pizza acrobats" who enter competitions and serve "as ambassadors of the USA pizza industry internationally." You want to see some serious pizza flipping and twirling action? Check out their videos.

▶ *uspizzateam.com*

Virtual Pizza Parlor. Fun and informative—you build your own pizza, choosing crust, sauce, and toppings, and find out, step by step, how many calories and how much fat, sodium, cholesterol, and fiber you're adding. Simple but effective.

▶ *http://people.bu.edu/salge/pizza/pizza/build_pizza.html*

The Web's First Japanese Pizza Page. A rundown of the pizzas available at Pizza Studio in Tokyo. Judging by the descriptions, it's probably a good thing there isn't a Second Japanese Pizza Page. The most popular pizza is the Prime (pepperoni, chopped beef, bacon, mushrooms, green peppers, onions). Normal enough. Then you go to the Seafood pizza, described as "the ideal taste of sea goodness and mayonnaise!"

▶ *http://chachich.com/mdchachi/jpizza.html*

World Pizza Champions. "America's #1 Pizza Team," and not to be confused with the U.S. Pizza Team. Founders include Tony Gemignani, an eight-time world champion "pizza

"For the first time ever, overweight people outnumber average people in America. Doesn't that make overweight the average, then? Last month you were fat, now you're average—hey, let's get a pizza!"
—Jay Leno

acrobat." Every year they invite the country's best pizza competitors and bakers to join them at the World Pizza Championships in Salsomaggiore, Italy.

▶ *worldpizzachampions.com*

Worstpizza.com. Dedicated, ironically, to finding the best pizza out there. Actually owned by the Pizza Experts, which does pizza marketing and public relations. Reviews of pizzerias around the country, with some interesting editor's notes—"management has since informed me that they have corrected the below Cheese Shaker issue by getting new ones."

▶ *worstpizza.com*

Web Zines

PizzaToday.com. Website for Louisville-based *Pizza Today*, "the most powerful marketing tool in the pizza industry." Loads of news, tips, and advice, plus video and a classified section, "Cheese Market News." *Pizza Today* hosts the International Pizza Expo, held annually in Las Vegas.

PMQ.com. Website for Oxford, Mississippi–based *PMQ Pizza Magazine*, "the #1 pizza trade magazine and official website of the pizza industry." News, trends, and tips, plus a "This Week in Pizza" weekly video feature, programs from Pizza Radio, an "Ask the Experts" column, and more.

FACT:
Americans eat about 250 million pounds of pepperoni on pizza every year.

Condiments, L&B Spumoni Gardens, Brooklyn.

Pizza Reviews

The Bronx

Best Italian Pizza, 202 East Fordham Road, (718) 562–5806. Talk about location; this handsome chrome-fronted storefront is located at the corner of Fordham Road and the Grand Concourse, right outside the Fordham Road B and D subway stop. Slices are $2, and they're immense. Considering the buffet-line look of the interior, they're acceptable. A dozen stools, no tables. Just ignore the clutter of napkins, straws, and paper on the floor; customers must have thought Mom was going to clean up their mess. Great people-watching spot at one of the city's liveliest crossroads.

Best Italian Pizza, the Bronx.

Captain's Table Pizzeria & Restaurant, 1056 Morris Park Avenue, (718) 824–5036. Five tables up front, dining room hidden from view, in back. Massive slices; serious bang for your pizza buck. The white is the cheesiest pizza of its kind I've seen anywhere—huge, almost otherworldly clumps of tasty ricotta. The marinara packs a nice garlic/oregano punch with a thick browned crunchy crust and an Italian grandma–worthy sauce.

Catania's Pizzeria & Cafe, 2305 Arthur Avenue, (718) 584–3583. "Home of the World Famous Sicilian Pizza and mini-calzone." Sicilians come in two varieties—regular and marinara. Friendly owner, Ronny. He took over the pizzeria in 1981; it opened down the street in 1949. Pleasant corner spot where Arthur Avenue begins. The cheese on the plain tasted a bit worn, but I liked the crunchy, whitish-brown crust. Loved the marinara Sicilian, with big swirls of plum tomatoes and topped with garlic. Most Sicilians in the city don't taste cooked all the way through; this one does. Begs for a nice glass of wine.

Crosby's Pizza Stop, 1731 Crosby Avenue, (718) 823–8980. Bright lights, pizza city; the lighting in this pleasantly divey hangout could hurt your eyes.

Bright orange booths—nine in all—add to the overall kitsch. Love the menu—entirely in black-and-white lettering. The plain slice is crisp, but that's about it, with a too-doughy crust. Known for its Sicilian. It's a slice above, with a buttery crust, crispy interior, and cheese drooping over the sides like it wants to escape. In a city of dreary assembly-line Sicilians, it stands out.

Classic black-and-white menu, Crosby's, the Bronx.

Cross Bronx Pizzeria, 2170 Cross Bronx Expressway, (718) 892–8459. Hey, you never know when your car will break down on the Cross Bronx and you'll crave a late-night slice while waiting for AAA. This white-walled pizza dive—it has all the charm of a bus stop at 3 in the morning—is actually located not on the Cross Bronx but on a street above and parallel to it. Two beat-up tables and half a dozen battered chairs add to the low-rent charm. Giant slices; amazingly, they're edible, especially late at night. Just close your eyes when you walk in.

Domenick's Pizza, 1015 Allerton Avenue, (718) 547–6171. Photos of Italian town scenes and local soccer teams on the wall. Interesting: The owners, Vito and Maria, change the pizzas daily. There are always plain and Sicilian slices, then shrimp and spinach or other intriguing combos. The plain is agreeably sloppy and gooey, with a nice distinct crisp. The Sicilian is a mouthful, with more excellent crunch, but the cheese is not something you can't find elsewhere.

Emilio's of Morris Park, 1051 Morris Park Avenue, (718) 822–6758. Home of the "frisbee"—small round focaccia filled with varying ingredients, changed daily. This day's frisbee—mozzarella, tomato, and eggplant. Seventies soundtrack—bring your disco outfit. The white slice is oily, but lively (nothing like a little oregano) and layered with good cheese. The marinara Sicilian is heavy on the herbs and doesn't taste fully cooked, but it's still enjoyable.

Famous Frank's Original Pizza, 2823 Middletown Road, (718) 597–3333. "Special for Lehman High school students only—two slices and soda, $5.50," reads a sign at this popular neighborhood pizzeria, across the street from Jerry's Soap Opera Laundromat. Two tables in front, dining room to side. Known for their Grandma, here called a Gran MaMa. The bottom is admirably crunchy, but tired-looking cheese on top ruins it. Infinitely better: the focaccia with red sauce. I'd rank that red sauce just behind Captain's Table; you'll want to dip a piece of bread, or your fingers, in it. The plain slice, good and oily, boasts a nice clean cheesy taste, with none of the rubbery texture or metallic aftertaste you find at many slice joints.

Famous Giovanni's, 2537 Webster Avenue, (718) 933–2125. There's just enough room in here for the four tables, four stools, and ATM machine. Amazingly, good pizza, on a stretch of street you'd least expect it—dollar stores, fast-food joints, cell phone shops. The sauce makes it—more tart than sweet, more fresh than anything. The Grandma is not too far behind. The best plain slice in the Fordham Road/Webster Avenue area, apart from Pugsley's.

Four Brothers Gyro Pizza, 18 East Gun Hill Road, (718) 405–7088. The gyro, thankfully, is separate from the pizza, although you can get a Jamaican meat pattie slice. Another pizza dive, with cracked tile floors and six tables hemmed in against the wall. Walk past the crates, mops, and an odd sneaker or two to reach the tiny bathroom in back. But wait a minute: It's a darned good slice, with a slightly burnt crust and a great crisp, and better than any of the slices in an all-day Queens trip the day before. The white slice looked wonderful, with its monstrous clumps of ricotta, but the cheese did not exactly taste fresh, and the crust is nowhere as memorable as the plain.

Full Moon Pizza, 600 East 187th Street, (718) 584–3451. Customer to guy behind counter: "You know Joey Numbers?" Sounds like Joey should have been on *The Sopranos.* At the corner of East 187th and Arthur Avenue, which seems to be the street of big slices; the plain at this busy pizzeria is a two-hander. It's as close to a thin crust as you'll get around here, with an ordinary top but firm, welcoming foundation. Pretty fair

square, with a fresh, tart, tomato sauce. TV screens everywhere, some tuned to sports, others showing the menu.

Giovanni Restaurant & Great Pizza, 80 West Fordham Road, (718) 733–3333. Now, that's a name. Curbside pickup available, which is a good thing, because there are only four booths. The only other place to rest your slice is atop the garbage can; two bus drivers were doing exactly that when I was there. OK plain slice, much better margherita. The basil looks like it ran the New York Marathon, but better-than-average cheese and sauce. Now I just need to find out why the box shows a lobster chasing the pizza delivery guy.

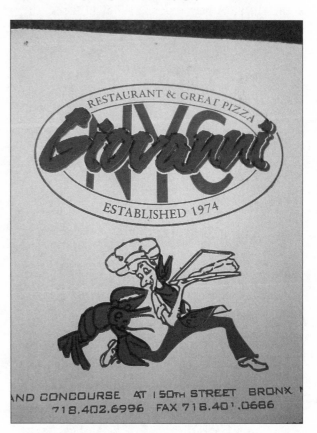

Giovanni Restaurant & Great Pizza, the Bronx.

131

Giovanni's, 2343 Arthur Avenue, (718) 933–4141. Half a dozen tables in takeout area up front; big dining room way in back. Giovanni gets around; there are photos of him with Bill Clinton, Hillary Clinton, Rudy Giuliani, and George Bush. The plain slice is standard issue, with unappealing brownish cheese. The focaccia saves the day. It's topped with a mini mountain of tomatoes, onions, and black olives, although they should take a class from Catania's; it's not cooked all the way through.

Ivana's Pizzeria, 2373 Arthur Avenue, (718) 365–4322. Funky-looking tables (just four) decorated with apples, oranges, grapefruit, and grapes. Small TV by the window and yellow neon moon sign. Giant slices; they may be the biggest in the Bronx. The plain tastes better than

it looks, with a wide, thick, eminently chewy crust. The Sicilian, as thick as a phone book, has a great crisp and pliant texture, but the cheese peels right off—big no-no—and there's nothing else special about it.

Joe's Pizza, 3009A Middletown Road, (718) 931–3145. First sighting of the Ruth Orkin photo "American Girl in Italy 1951"—it seems to be in every pizzeria in Jersey. Red-plastic-tablecloth-topped tables. Different always counts in the cookie-cutter pizza business, and the marinara (no cheese) slice stands out, with its sprinkle of garlic, basil, and olive oil. The Sicilian also breaks from the pack—solid crust, more sauce than usual, pleasant crunch. "Best Pizza in Town," say the awning and menu. Joe's is right up there.

Louie & Ernie's Pizza, 1300 Crosby Avenue, (718) 829–6230. For cool factor, this subterranean pizza joint is tough to beat. It's located squarely in the middle of a residential neighborhood; look for the bright neon sign. Walk several steps down to the cramped front counter and place your takeout order, or grab a table in what looks like someone's den. Wood paneling, fast-talking waitresses, and Yankees-cap-wearing customers complete the family atmosphere. Well, well—a plain slice with attitude. It's floppy and oily and uneven around the edges—like someone tore off a piece—and packed with flavor. The Sicilian, coated with an Antarctica-rated cheesy blanket, is not as memorable as the plain; Joe's on Middletown Road does it better. The guy behind the counter apologizes several times for overlooking me. "Gonna stay, babe?" he asks later. A must-stop on any Bronx—any city-wide—pizza field trip.

Majestic Pizza, 16 West Fordham Road, (718) 933–3050. "Real Italian pizza" advertised on window. It's really not. The crust is barely cooked and tastes like unfinished bread. The rest isn't awful, just blindingly mediocre. No tables, but ten black stools along a ledge. Maybe you'll do better with the Majestic Special—"Pizza Pie. $5.00. All Day! Every Day!"

Mario's Pizzeria & Restaurant, 79 East Gun Hill Road, (718) 231–3086. Nothing like the pungent smell

Massive Sicilian, Mario's Pizzeria & Restaurant, the Bronx.

of ammonia to accompany your slice; the guy mopping the floor slams the wood garbage receptacle against the wall and looks pretty angry at something; the manager tells him to go home. Decent plain slice; not as good as Charlie's or Four Brothers, but good enough. Thickest Sicilian in the city? Here's a contender. It's so massive you can barely fit your mouth around it. More bread than pizza, and could use a sauce transfusion.

The Original Three Boys from Italy Pizzeria,

704 Burke Avenue, (718) 882–2009. Open-late neighborhood pizza joint with just four tables, lots of floor space, and all sorts of messages and rules— "We Will Charge You Tax When We Ring Up Your Bill," "Absolutely" no soda to be brought in from the outside, no ice, etc. Good plain slice; you may wish for a bit more sauce, but it does the job, especially late at night. Grab a couple slices and walk up the steps to the Burke Avenue subway stop, right outside the door.

Paesano's Pizza & Pasta, 330 East 188th Street,

(347) 590–6616. Green-and-red neon tubing; TV tuned to teen channel one minute, police car chases on TruTV the next. Divey-looking, but the Sicilian is surprisingly acceptable, with a genuine crust and decent cheese. Wish there were more sauce, but I won't complain too much. The colorful mural of the pizza maker on the side of the building is worth a look, and a photo.

Pizza Corner & Pasta, 769 Allerton Avenue,

(718) 798–5507. Familiar orange booths (who invented them, and why orange?). Biggest pizza box anywhere on display here—it's used for the Party Pie, thirty-two slices, about $40. The plain slice is hefty, with a hint of onion, and a good sauce, if you can find it. The imposing Sicilian looks like it weighs five pounds. More bread than pizza, and bland besides.

Pugsley's Pizza, 590 East 191st Street,

(718) 365–0327. Practically hidden on a side street just outside the Fordham University gates, Pugsley's is one of the city's most unique pizzerias, with its wooden-beamed booths, diner-like front counter, a table fashioned from a piece of sidewalk, various inspirational messages, a sculpted Statue of Liberty, and nutty owner Sal Natale. The plain makes for a simple, classic New York slice—the cheese, crust, and sauce all working together like a well-written term paper.

Roma Pizza, 1300 Castle Hill Avenue,

(718) 597–8330. How can you resist a pizzeria that describes itself as "Home of the Toppings"? Well, you can. Located practically under the No. 6 train platform, the American-flag-decorated Roma offers every imaginable chicken-pizza combination—chicken with broccoli, chicken cutlet, chicken cutlet parmigiana, and, well, you get the idea. The Sicilian should be promptly sent back to Sicily, or better yet, a trash can; the cheese looks like it was dropped from a great height. The lasagna pizza bears no resemblance to lasagna or pizza; the cheese has the consistency of thickened wasabi paste. There's a Papa John's a half block away. Just sayin'.

University Pizza & Restaurant, 574 East Fordham

Road, (718) 220–1959. Charmless pizzeria with orange walls and five booths. The green-and-red neon sign is the main attraction. The grade for this university pizza? C minus—you didn't flunk, but you don't want your mom to see the report card. The crust is way too soft and chewy; a little crunch would be a game-changer. Gummy-tasting, but edible in a pulling-an-all-nighter sort of way.

Brooklyn

Albanese Pizza & Restaurant, 412 Fifth Avenue, Park Slope, (718) 369–2767. Situated on too-cool-for-school Fifth Avenue (cute cafes, retro shops, even a superhero supply store). But the plain slice here needs to disappear, and the tomatoes on the Sophia Loren (also with mozzarella and garlic) looked past their expiration date. Plenty of pizza options, including nine kinds of pan pizzas, not exactly a Brooklyn staple. Just-average pizza, but I love the "Elvis Live at the Florida Theater" sign.

Anna Maria Pizza, 179 Bedford Avenue, Williamsburg, (718) 599–4550. Smudged walls, tile floors, worn/torn green chairs, and photos of the Three Stooges, the Beatles, and Al Pacino on the wall. Plenty of choices in the pizza department, most loaded with toppings. If you like mondo-oily plain slices, you're in heaven, although the rest of the slice will bring you right back down to earth. The Sicilian is different in shape— it's sliced in triangles—but the rest is hauntingly familiar.

Bergen Pizza, 67 Sixth Avenue, Prospect Heights, (718) 636–4863. Funky color scheme, even for a pizzeria: walls painted beige on the upper half, green and maroon on the lower. Striking mural of fishing boats bobbing in water. Monstrous plain slice—one of the five biggest in Brooklyn—but tasteless and mushy-crusted, and the cheese looks like it had been applied over a period of days. And the square tasted like it was cooked in an Easy-Bake Oven. The business card, showing the fishing boat mural, is way better than the pizza.

Best Pizza, 33 Havemeyer Street, Williamsburg, (718) 599–2210. Simple classic facade—"Best Pizza" sign glowing warmly in the night. Hardwood floors, well-worn wooden booths, six tables, rap music playing—and the city's only paper plate art gallery, as far as I know. Customers draw/scrawl images and messages on plates; scores are taped to the walls and ceiling, testimonials to Best's goodness. "Yum to the tum," "I ate the thing," "bitchin pizza," "P.S. 214 pizza club," and more. One plate has "Gawd" written on it eight times. The plain slice is cheesy, seasoned, basil-topped; you'll love the crisp. Intriguing Grandma—puffy, crusty, buttery top, almost a baked effect. A singular, one-of-a-kind Grandma. Girl walks in, asks for a slice. "Did it just come out?" she says, excitement in her voice. Best Pizza: the best plain slice in Williamsburg.

Brooklyn Pizza, 717 Fulton Street, Fort Greene, (718) 625–4499. Mobbed by schoolkids in midafternoon. Why? Plain slices are only a buck from 2 to 5 P.M. weekdays. Bonus: You don't have to be a kid to get that price. Decent slice, but it would have been improved immeasurably if it were hot and fully cooked. Failing grades on both.

Paper plate art, Best Pizza, Williamsburg.

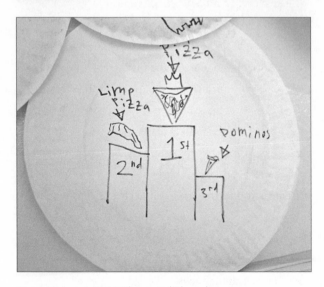

Sign inside Campo de Fiori, Brooklyn.

Campo de Fiori, 187 Fifth Avenue, Park Slope, (347) 763–0933. Classy but casual pizza cafe, with bottles of wine and cookbooks on the shelves and a collage on the wall that includes Marcello Mastroianni, Claudia Cardinale, and Sophia Loren (from Naples, the birthplace of modern pizza). "We speak Italian very well," says one sign. Owner Andrea PalMonte claims to offer the city's only "Roman-style" pizza (made with dough leavened for twenty-four hours, cold-pressed extra-virgin olive oil, and San Marzano tomatoes), but there are others. Creative choices here. A slice with roasted red peppers, finely chopped mushrooms, and onions is thoroughly enjoyable. The owner's daughter explains there's a better grade of mozzarella on the margherita, but I don't taste the difference. It's a nice slice, though; wish the sauce packed more personality.

Carmine's Pizzeria & Restaurant, 358 Graham Avenue, Williamsburg, (718) 782–9659. They sure love their Yankees here. Photos of Babe Ruth at his last game, player pictures in black-and-white and color, and a stadium photo signed by the likes of Joe Pepitone and

Paper plate art, Best Pizza, Williamsburg.

135

Tommy John. Only clue to the restroom: the "Be alert for foul balls" sign. The plain slice easily beats nearby Sal's; it's got more flavor, more life. It's a bit greasy, but you'll get over it. Cheese peels away in clumps on the Grandma/square—even a four-year-old pizza lover knows it shouldn't do that—but the nice sauce reminds me of the kind you'd put in your favorite lasagna.

Caruso's Pizzeria & Restaurant, 150 Smith Street, Cobble Hill, (718) 797–2300. No relation to the forgettable Caruso's in Penn Station. The burnt-cheese plain slice doesn't look too inviting, but it features an agreeable, slightly chewy crust. The square and a round marinara with pesto make nowhere near the same impression as the plain.

Casanova Restaurant & Pizzeria, 338 McGuinness Boulevard, Greenpoint, (718) 389–0990. Takeout section/bar up front, ten tables in back dining room. Dutiful cheese on the plain, but a distinctive crust with a bit of char. The margherita: another slightly charred crust and big clumps of tomatoes and bushels of basil. One of the better slices in this neighborhood.

Di Fara Pizza, 1424 Avenue J, Midwood, (718) 258–1367. This legendary Brooklyn pizzeria achieved notoriety in the summer of 2009 when it started charging $5 a slice, the city's first five-buck slice. Is it worth it? The Di Fara experience certainly is. Walk to the counter and place your order; Margaret Mieles, daughter of owner Dom DeMarco, will write it down on a yellow legal pad. And be prepared to wait; DeMarco makes his pizzas one by painstaking one, seemingly oblivious of the lines and anxious faces. The plain slice is a slightly charred, basil-topped wonder, oozing extra-virgin olive oil. Is it worth five bucks? Let me put it this way—I'd rather eat one slice here than two $2.50 slices at 90 percent of the pizzerias in the city.

Empire Slices, 298 Irving Avenue, Bushwick, (347) 404–7945. What is probably the city's smallest pizza joint—two chairs wedged into a Munchkin-sized space—serves a credible dollar slice, despite the pizzas being outnumbered by the honey bars at the counter. The sauce is on the sweet side, but the rest of the slice doesn't embarrass itself.

Fascati Pizza, 80 Henry Street, Brooklyn Heights, (718) 237–1278. Several blocks from Grimaldi's, and a lot easier to get into. Dizzy, delightful pizza art from Arturo Rosales on the brick walls. The plain is saucy, or saucy enough, with good cheese and an agreeably oily sheen. More good cheese on the white slice, although the crust is not as crispy, or as pleasing, as the plain. Press lightly on both slices and a pool of oil bubbles to the surface.

Forcella La Pizza DiNapoli, 485 Lorimer Street, Williamsburg, (718) 388–8820. Well-lit, brick-walled, hardwood-floored dining room with wooden tables and a blues soundtrack. Framed certificates attest to owner Guilio Adriani's standing in the pizza world; he won high honors for his margherita D.O.C. in the Pizza World Cup. Fried pizza may not sound especially tasty or practical, but the montanara, a fried margherita, is a pizza sensory experience: lightly fried crust and clumps of mozzarella, although a surfeit of sauce. The Calzone pizza bears no resemblance to the cheese-and-dough bombs at your local pizzeria; here the dough is blackened around the edges and filled with smoked mozzarella, sopressata, and ricotta. The whole charred gooey mess is an unqualified delight.

Fornino, 187 Bedford Avenue, Williamsburg, (718) 384–6004. Warm, cozy brick-walled retreat from Williamsburg's bustle. Dig the larger-than-life photos of tomatoes, corn, and peppers under the glass-topped tables. Tin ceiling; it's the upscale pizzeria's ceiling of choice. Some pizza makers shun bufala mozzarella because it tends to make the pizza soupy; that's exactly what happens to the margherita D.O.C. here. The fresh basil gives it a fragrance and feistiness, but otherwise it's not remarkable. The carciofo e salsiccia, meanwhile, is a hit; the fennel sausage and artichoke hearts, plus a heavenly combination of mozzarella and ricotta, resulted in one of my favorite pizzas anywhere.

Francesco's, 531 Henry Street, Carroll Gardens, (718) 834–0863. If you're looking for a much cheaper alternative to Lucali's, visit this yellow-walled neighborhood pizzeria just down the street. The margherita is good and crispy, but otherwise nothing special. A spinach/sausage white slice—intriguing combo—features big chunks of better-than-average sausage.

Franklin Pizza, 109 Franklin Street, Greenpoint, (718) 349–2472. Cool-looking pizzeria, with brick walls, New Age-y paintings, tin ceiling, mosaic tile. A Ronson Roto-Shine Magnetic Shoe Polisher sits atop the Pepsi cooler; it has nothing to do with pizza, but it's a nice retro touch. You don't see too many mushroom-only slices in the city; there's one here. The 'shrooms are not exactly imported, but they're a cut above the usual fished-out-of-the-giant-plastic-tub variety. Decent plain slice.

Franny's, 348 Flatbush Avenue, Park Slope, (718) 230–0221. I love the system here to keep track of customers and determine waiting time for a table; the manager marks down whether each table has just been seated, ordered an appetizer, ordered dinner, etc. And she'll scribble a short description of the person under whose name the table is being held; yours truly merited a "pelon," for bald. Friendly, helpful staff. What's with the real knives at each table? The pizzas are not sliced; Franny's is one of a handful of pizzerias with unsliced pies. The clams/chilies/parsley pizza had a shortage of chilies, and personality. But we really liked the tomato, mozzarella, and sausage pizza; the pepperoni-shaped thin sausage, often a sign of inferior meat, is good quality and works well with the other ingredients.

Gino's Pizzeria & Restaurant, 218 Flatbush Avenue, Prospect Heights, (718) 230–3932. Dig the crazy decor—multicolored triangles on white walls; it looks like the play zone at a pizza-only McDonald's, if such a thing ever came to pass. Another big bland slice, but at least the cheese tastes halfway fresh. The fresh mozzarella slice is a mistake—starter crust, faded tomato sauce. They literally roll out the red carpet here—a long red carpet with a smiling pizza maker, faded from years of use.

Grandma Rose's Pizza, 457 Graham Avenue, Williamsburg, (718) 389–1908. Grandma Rose's is one of the city's more unusually situated pizzerias, nestled right under the BQE at Our Lady of the Snows Square. There's a painting of Rose, grandmother of owner John Ricco, holding a tomato pie; she passed away in 1995. It's not pizza here, it's "abeetz," and according to the black stencil lettering in the window, it's "homemade on site." Old-school choices include an upside-down square, a Grandma, and a Svincioni Square (caramelized onions, bread crumbs, and grated cheese). The plain slice doesn't stand out, at least in this neighborhood. The square, supremely tomatoey, is the way to go.

Grimaldi's, 1 Front Street, DUMBO, (718) 858–4300. When owner Ralph Ciolli was evicted from Grimaldi's Old Fulton Street location in late 2011 for falling behind on city taxes and rent, he ended up next door, in a handsome 1869 building that was once Brooklyn's first safety deposit bank. The space is bigger, but you're still likely to wait in line for a table. Maybe no other pizzeria in the city evokes such love and hate as Grimaldi's. Old-timers lament the absence of Patsy Grimaldi, who came out of retirement to open Juliana's in the former Grimaldi's this year; others say it's Brooklyn's—or New York's—best pizza, no matter who's making it. With all the hype and hoopla, I thought I'd be disappointed, but the half plain/half sausage is a classic New York pizza with above-average sauce and cheese. For the full experience, order one to go (pizzas are placed, old-school style, in brown paper bags) and grab a table or bench in the waterfront park several blocks away.

A Grimaldi's pizza and the Brooklyn Bridge: perfect together.

Henry's Pizzeria, 1520 Myrtle Avenue, Bushwick, (718) 418–1107. Some places you visit for everything but the pizza; this is one of them. Dig the cartoon characters painted on the wall—Popeye holding a sub, Bugs Bunny with a mustard container, Betty Boop with what appears to be a pizza. The wall is plastered with photos of not-so-appetizing-looking food. Which brings us to the plain slice: decent crust, but wan-looking cheese and worse sauce. There's a $5 fourteen-inch pizza, if you're on a budget and don't put a premium on taste.

House of Pizza and Calzone, 132 Union Street, Carroll Gardens, (718) 624–9107. Crazy-thick hardwood floors with ruts and ridges; you'll feel like you're in a stable, or a cabin in the woods. There's a fifteen-foot-long counter where you can do pizza stand-up; four tables, then a brick-walled dining room out back. Beyond that, an outdoor patio with picnic tables. The entire space is big enough for a wedding reception or two. Grease is the word here; the plain slice is crispy, nicely burnt, and greasy-good. The Sicilian boasts a nice semi-tart sauce and an uber-crispy crust, but it's too bready and insubstantial inside.

Il Porto Ristorante Wood Brick-Oven Pizza, 37 Washington Avenue, Clinton Hill, (718) 624–0954. Attractive brick-walled space, with takeout and several tables on one side and spacious dining room on the other. Your grandma doesn't rock like the Grandma pizza here. Bursting with tomatoey color and flavor, it's one of the ten best in the city. The Supreme pizza, with crushed tomatoes, homemade mozzarella, basil, and Parmigiano, may be even better. Il Porto was a hit; I'd return in a New York minute.

Italy Pizza, 800 Manhattan Avenue, Greenpoint, (718) 383–9079. Squarely in the middle of Greenpoint's practically all-Polish section—markets, delis, restaurants, travel agencies. Narrow counter up front, five tables and six stools in back. Painting of Marlon Brando on the wall with the words: "I'll make you a pizza you can't refuse." Well, you can refuse the white pizza—seriously oily, and tastes undercooked. The marinara with onion and garlic sauce: another unfinished/undercooked crust, but a tart tomatoey sauce.

J&V Pizzeria, 6322 Eighteenth Avenue, Bensonhurst, (718) 232–2700. "Famous pizza since 1950" and "home of the JoJo sandwich" ("chicken or meatball on garlic bread"). Founded by Johnny Mortillaro (from Sicily) and Vinny DeGrezia (from Naples), who "were responsible for introducing the idea of selling pizza by the slice." There's a book in all the claims made by pizzerias around the city alone. In any event, it's a no-frills slice joint with plenty of charm. The Grandma is seriously saucy, with a good sauce, one of my favorite anywhere. The bland crust, though, didn't seem worthy.

Joe's Pizza of the Village, 349 Fifth Avenue, Park Slope, (718) 832–2525. The owner worked in Joe's on Carmine Street in the Village; to show his "respect and gratitude" he decided to name his place "Joe's Pizza of the Village." Another schoolkid haunt; it's right across the street from a middle school. Red-framed doors, brick walls, and a walk-up sidewalk window. The plain looks like the same classic thin slice you get at the original Joe's, but something seems to have been lost in the translation. The white is the way to go: creamy cheese you'll be licking off with your fingers. Well, I did, anyway.

Joe's Pizzeria, 259 Prospect Park West, Windsor Terrace, (718) 965–3433. Neighborhood slice joint. Bland cheese, too-soft crust, and unsurprising sauce add up to pizza with little flavor and character.

Johnny's Original Pizzeria, 436 New Lots Avenue, East New York, (718) 272–5755. "Staying with some guy, lost my job, scoping the neighborhood, looking for a good pizzeria," says a guy in his sixties with a slice talking to someone on his cell about insurance. Johnny's is that kind of place: sagging ceiling, fluorescent-lit bare walls, the space large enough to play half-court basketball. The plain tastes better than it looks; chalk one up to the wonders of oregano. Only three choices the day I visited: plain, pepperoni, and chicken.

Johnny's Original Pizzeria, East New York.

L&B Spumoni Gardens, 2725 86th Street, Gravesend, (718) 449–1230. Belongs on any list of ten must-visit New York City pizzerias, whether you like Sicilian, its

139

Interior, L&B Spumoni Gardens, Brooklyn.

Sign, L&B Spumoni Gardens, Brooklyn.

Kristin Federico about to sample the Sicilian at L&B Spumoni Gardens, Brooklyn.

trademark pizza, or not. It's an experience like no other: grab a couple slices inside and sit down at one of the metal picnic tables outside. To the right is a sit-down restaurant, with separate bathrooms (patio customers are supposed to use the bathrooms around the corner from the takeout window). In between the pizza and the restaurant is the ice cream/spumoni counter. Whole pizzas are called Sicilian, but when it comes time to order a slice, don't act like a tourist; ask for a "square" slice. The plain "round" slice here is ordinary. The square comes as a slight disappointment considering all the hype heaped on it. But it's still a commendable slice; the best thing going for it is the sauce. The undercooked layer of dough underneath? Somebody was in a rush. Chill out with some of the excellent spumoni.

La Piazza Pizzeria, 229 Prospect Park West, Windsor Terrace, (718) 499–0006. The menu says Park Slope, although *Yelp* and other sites put it in Windsor Terrace. Interesting slices—an all mushroom, an all black olive, a white focaccia, and a burrata, with that creamy cheese, freshly chopped tomatoes, and extra-virgin olive oil. At

"midnight madness"—11:30 to midnight Friday and Saturday—everything is $1. The Al Funghi boasted quality regular and portobello mushrooms, but the cheese tasted like it had been sitting on the pizza too long. The margherita, with mozzarella, "two-blend cheese," San Marzano tomato sauce, and pecorino Romano grated cheese, is acceptable.

Lenny's Pizzeria, 594 Fifth Avenue, Park Slope, (718) 788–8928. "The best Italian pizza in Brooklyn," the menu proclaims of Lenny's, open since 1954. Modest,

140

aren't we? Brick wall on one side, tiled wall on the other, Formica-topped counter, wood paneling in back: seems like they have all the pizzeria design bases covered. The plain slice is just too oily/greasy. The margherita looked promising, but it's bad news: the cheese tasted off, and the basil on top might have been from 1954.

Lucali's, 575 Henry Street, Carroll Gardens, (718) 858–4086. You can't get much closer to the pizza makers, at least at a high-end pizzeria, than here. A tub of Calabro ricotta stands ready on the table, a pizza maker with a Rolling Stones Sticky Fingers T-shirt is busy forming and stretching the dough. Hardwood floors, logs of wood on a chair, a vintage Coca-Cola sign and a fifties house music soundtrack add to the retro/rustic interior. The pizzas come out fast, even for a near-full house. The crusts are among the city's puffiest—airy, hollow constructions. There is no menu as such; the waitress gives you the available toppings, and you go from there. A half marinara, with top-flight ingredients, may be by the numbers, but the numbers add up. Artichokes and shallots, on the other half, prove to be a winning combination. You decide whether it's all worth the $30 price tag.

Luigi's Pizza, 686 Fifth Avenue, Park Slope, (718) 499–3857. Menu board reminiscent of a 1950s drive-in movie snack bar; cash register probably older than that. Small; just six tables. Voted best Brooklyn slice by worstpizza.com and "King of Kings" by the *Daily News.* Love the paintings of Coney Island—Wonder Wheel, boardwalk games of chance—on the wall. The Grandma pizza is seriously drippy/oily/buttery; I wanted to like it more than I did. Good garlicky red sauce on the fresh mozzarella/tomato sauce pizza, but I expected more overall, considering the acclaim.

Luigi's Pizzeria, 326 DeKalb Avenue, Clinton Hill, (718) 783–2430. No tables, and barely enough room for four, five people. Love the faded movie posters—*Moonstruck, Serpico, Lords of Flatbush,* others. Autographed photo from Dom DeLuise, for whatever that's worth. Much better plain slice than nearby Mario's; the cheese tastes like cheese, and there's a modest crunch to the crust, but immodest oily slippage. The Sicilian looked and tasted as if it had been sitting out too long; the tasty sauce made up for lackluster cheese.

Mario's Pizza, 224 DeKalb Avenue, Fort Greene, (718) 260–9520. Fluorescent-lit pizza dive; no tables, just five tattered red stools along a red ledge and mirrored wall. The twelve faded pizzas on the wall chart are symbolic of the real pizzas here—fair cheese, insubstantial crust, and in need of a modern makeover.

Nina's Pizzeria & Restaurant, 635 Meeker Avenue, Greenpoint, (718) 389–8854. Below-average plain slice, with off-color cheese blotting. The marinara is hefty, but here size doesn't matter; the sauce needs an overhaul.

Not Ray's Leo's Pizza, 2726 Mermaid Avenue, Coney Island, (718) 996–5575. More Rays! Photos of Ray Charles, Sugar Ray Leonard, Ray Liotta, Ray Lewis, and Ray Romano adorn the walls, yet the names of the Rays on the takeout menu are crossed out. Divey Coney Island pizzeria. The Russian-accented guy behind the counter calls you "boss," and plain slices are just two bucks. They won't make much of an impression unless you're dying of hunger, but you can't beat the price. The margherita is oily, but its pert red sauce and tasty flour-dusted crust make it better than most of the margheritas in slice joints out there.

Two Not Ray's pizzerias, Brooklyn.

Not Ray's Pizza, 690 Fulton Street, Fort Greene, (718) 855–8206. Rays on display: actor Ray Milland (a still from *The Big Clock*), director Ray Harryhausen, singer Johnnie Ray. They really have their Rays covered here; there are also vintage photos of Famous Original Ray's Pizza, World Famous Ray's Pizza, World's Famous Ray's Pizza & Pasta, and Ray Bari Pizza. Whew. It's an artistic corner: The building across the street houses Habana Outpost, with its bright blue-green facade, while the side of Not Ray's building is covered with a two-story-high mural of rapper Biggie Smalls—here portrayed as Comandante Biggie. The plain is a decent hot slice; it smells better than it tastes. The margherita comes as a sweet surprise, balanced and seasoned, even if the crust is kind of nowhere.

Paulie Gee's, 60 Greenpoint Avenue, Greenpoint, (347) 987–4747. Paul Giannone, who started making pizzas in a backyard oven behind his Jersey home, opened his "pizza joint" in March 2010 to much fanfare. Sixties and seventies rock music provides the house soundtrack—don't go here expecting a quiet romantic

evening. And don't walk behind the counter: The kitchen and oven are off-limits to customers, even reporters. Try the Delboy, with fior di latte, Italian tomatoes, Berkshire sopressata picante, and Parmigiano-Reggiano. The sauce may be spread too thin for some. The signature pizza is the Greenpointer, with fior di latte, baby arugula, olive oil, fresh lemon juice, and shaved Parmigiano-Reggiano. Quality ingredients, excellent pizza, fun place, good beer selection.

Peppino's Brick Oven Pizza & Restaurant, 469 Fifth Avenue, Park Slope, (718) 768–7244. Only one kind of slice was available when I stopped—a plain—but it's a keeper. Someone actually reached for the herbs and spices and gave a plain some life. It's thin crust, with moderate blackening at the edges. With its stock decor—red vintage tablecloths, photos of Marilyn Monroe and the Brooklyn Bridge—you don't expect much, but Peppino's delivers. If the crust had been crispier, it would be a super slice.

Pizza Cotta-Bene, 291 Third Avenue, Gowanus, (718) 722–7200. Attractive brick-walled restaurant with a framed photo of Sinatra from his 1981 album *She Shot Me Down*. Choices include a margherita with and without tomatoes, an upside-down pizza, and both Grandma (mozzarella, fresh basil, plum tomato sauce) and Grandpa (mozzarella, basil, vodka sauce) pies. The plain is pleasing, but you'd expect better considering the name and surroundings. The margherita, in any case, is an improvement, with a crisp crust.

Pizza on the Run, 2914 Stillwell Avenue, Coney Island, (718) 513–0454. Across the street from the Coney Island subway station. They don't want you lingering, apparently; there are no tables and just two stools inside. A bank of security cameras is positioned above a stack of pizza boxes. There's a walk-up sidewalk counter, and the stainless-steel-topped garbage can outside serves as a makeshift table; it worked for me. The plain slice—just $2—may be the biggest in Brooklyn. The Grandma is garlicky and the cheese pulls off like a bad wig, but overall it's not disagreeable. "Are you a journalist?" asks a girl. "How did you know?" "I saw the camera." "Lots of people carry cameras." "I saw the notebook." "You got me there." Her boyfriend jumped in: "What kind of question is that, are you a journalist? What else would you ask—are you a crack dealer?"

Sidewalk scene, Pizza on the Run, Coney Island.

Box, Pizza on the Run, Coney Island.

Princess Pizzeria & Restaurant, 535 Fifth Avenue, Park Slope, (718) 788–9111. Pizzeria as Long Island diner; maroon booths and more mirrored glass than the average banquet hall. CPR kit message points somewhere in the direction of the bathroom. The crust on the plain slice—airy, crackly—is far more memorable than the cheese or sauce. The white pizza, with good-enough ricotta, is marred by a layer of uncooked dough.

Roberta's, 261 Moore Street, Bushwick, (718) 417–1118. Sweep aside the curtains at the front entrance and step into the bustling beer-hall-like dining room, or proceed to a smaller dining room to the left of the always-packed bar, or the army tent outside that doubles as an open-year-round tiki bar. The craft beer selection is engagingly eclectic, and you can get cans of Bud to go for $3. Roberto's has gained renown for its overall menu (pasta, lamb breast, pork chop, skirt steak, etc.) but the formidable oven up front stays busy cranking out pizzas. The Rosso (tomato, oregano, garlic) teases with a tasty sauce, but it's spread too thin. The R.P.S., with tomato, mozzarella, sopressata picante, and roasted red pepper, is a slippery, sliding success.

Rocco's Famous Pizzeria & Ristorante, 522 Neptune Avenue, Coney Island, (718) 996–8839. Red/green neon tubing, peach walls, fourteen tables. Russian spoken here; many customers from neighboring Brighton Beach. The usual photos of the Manhattan skyline and Frank Sinatra, plus a painting of construction workers atop a high-rise girder, with Sylvester Stallone, pizza box in hand, swinging on a rope. Probably the best slice on Coney Island (remember, Totonno's does whole pizzas only), with a touch of oregano, the oil pleasantly pooling. The square, though, looked sickly, and it wasn't because of the funky lighting.

Russ Pizza, 745 Manhattan Avenue, Greenpoint, (718) 383–9463. I liked the decor—orange tables, tile floors, crucifixes along mirrored walls, a bas-relief of Pope Paul. Standard slice, though: decent crust, below-average sauce. The Grandma is better, with its oniony sauce. But the cheese peels off; not good.

Sal's Pizzeria, 544 Lorimer Street, Williamsburg, (718) 599–7032. Popular, packed neighborhood hangout; parents and kids abound. When I ask, "Can I have a receipt if possible?" the guy behind the counter replies, "Anything is possible here." The plain is just that. The square boasts a nice crispy foundation but tastes like graham crackers meets Keebler, or something like that. Wish pizzeria owners would stop putting extra cheese atop the Grandma; leave Grandma alone!

Sam's Restaurant and Pizzeria, 238 Court Street, Cobble Hill, (718) 596–3458. Open since 1930, and one of the city's most iconic old-school Italian restaurants. Booths and bar in front; a dining room out back that looks like an American Legion hall. Owner Lou Migliaccio talks about Cousin Tony and Uncle Danny and a couple aunts and his father Mario and other family members; after a while I couldn't keep track of who was who. But the pizza is first-rate, with a pleasant, almost fragrant red sauce (they use Alta Cucina whole plum tomatoes) and a charred, not too crunchy crust. Worth a visit for the pizza and the experience.

San Marco Pizzeria, 577 Lorimer Street, Williamsburg, (718) 387–4861. Opened in 1969 by Cono and Domenic Manzolillo, and scarcely seems to have changed since then: faded walls, high ceiling, four tables, five stools; a time-warp place you can escape to. The plain is a better-than-average slice, with a distinctive

crisp bottom. The square packs a good crunchy crust and welcome seasoning, but the cheese looks like it's calcified.

Saraghina, 435 Halsey Street, Bedford-Stuyvesant, (718) 574–0010. Pizzeria with a bohemian sensibility and decor by way of a yard sale, with chairs hanging from the ceiling and a vintage *McCall's Cookbook* and metal airplanes made from spray cans in the men's room. Two dining rooms; try to get seated in the smaller, quieter room adjoining the coffee/takeout area. The pizza boxes (the imprint of a fork, knife, and spoon on an otherwise plain brown box) and business cards (faded-ink name and address printed on index cards) continue the lack of pretense. The prosciutto/funghi pizza is loaded with both; the mushrooms are especially tasty, and the overall result is highly recommended. The salsiccia pizza combines sausage and kalamata olives, a match made in my pizza heaven, although the sausage is on the greasy side.

The 3 Luigis, 275 Grand Avenue, Clinton Hill, (718) 622–0059. Sister store to Luigi's on DeKalb Avenue, and a major upgrade in decor: hardwood floors and eight tables of varying sizes. There is only one Luigi—Luigi Viaggio; he, his brother, and Rosario Longo are the co-owners. Omar Epps delivered pizzas here for a while. More *Serpico* posters. The margherita combines a sweet sauce and crunchy crust. The marinara featured good tomatoes, but not-so-good browned cheese.

Toby's Public House, 686 Sixth Avenue, South Slope, (718) 788–1186. Cozy bar with brick oven in back. A dozen chairs at the bar, ten tables. The washroom—that's what it's labeled—is wedged between the ATM machine and a countertop. Eclectic craft beer selection, including

Little Sumpin' Ale, Bit Burger Pilsner, Blue Point Rastafa Ale, and "Toby's Cheap Beer." Varied pizza choices, including spicy pecorino, smoked pancetta, Tartufata (black truffle cream sauce, crimini, prosciutto cotto), and the Del Macellaio (tomato, mozzarella, sausage, red onion). The Bufalina D.O.C., with buffalo mozzarella, tomato, basil, and olive oil, is excellent; I resisted the urge to eat the whole pizza before leaving. I'd definitely go back—for the pizza, the beer, and the vibe.

Tony's Pizza & Pasta, 355 Graham Avenue, Williamsburg, (718) 384–8669. Across the street from Carmine's. No-nonsense guy behind counter: "What else?" and "Anything else?" Message on T-shirts: "Big Tony's—if you like my meatballs you'll like my sausage" and "The best meat in your mouth." Sign on door: "No no no. No pets allowed." Unfortunate brownish cheese on the plain, but a winning crispy crust. The upside-down marinara is formidable-looking, but the sauce is not even on the level of Ragu.

Totonno's, 1524 Neptune Avenue, Coney Island, (718) 372–8606. You know just by looking at a pizza that's it's going to be good? Totonno's is that kind of pizza. The white is simple, and simply a classic, a near-perfect blend of cheese and crust. The red is just as good, with a real homemade taste in the not-too-tart, not-too-sweet sauce, and excellent cheese. It's amazing how many New Yorkers I encountered in my travels who had never been to Totonno's. Hop on the D, N, F, or Q train and go. Now.

Triangolo Pizza, 1017 Manhattan Avenue, Greenpoint, (718) 389–5885. Photos of local soccer teams on the walls, plus one of Steven Seagal and a license plate reading 9/11/01. T-shirts read, "Make pizza, not war."

Faded wood-paneled walls; open-air in warmer months. Menu advertises locations in Napoli, Palermo, and New York. The plain is slightly better than average. The Sicilian, long and rectangular, looks like a cheese torpedo. It's not the bomb, but it's better than the plain.

Val Diano, 659 Manhattan Avenue, Greenpoint, (718) 383–1707. Four glass-topped tables up front; dining room in back that looks like it hasn't changed in forty years, with a Sunday afternoon blue-hair crowd. Plain slice didn't look promising on the pan, but the wonders of reheating revived it. Best part: the crust, supple and chewy. The white is better: a pleasant browned baked top and an airy, crackly crust.

Verde Coal Oven, 254 Irving Avenue, Bushwick, (718) 381–8800. When Charlie Verde acquired this building on Irving Avenue, which housed a bakery in the early 1900s, he found a surprise in the basement— the bakery's original coal-fired brick oven. He restored the oven, and it remains in the basement, which is why the slogan here is "Where the pizza is made right under your feet!" It's a supremely cozy little pizza cafe, with hardwood floors, green-checked tablecloths, and loaves of ciabatta, whole wheat sourdough, and more on the shelves. The marinara is, well, different—thin, crackery/buttery-crusted. The sauce in a marinara should stand out; this one doesn't. Better: the margherita, with a more noticeable crisp and crunch, the basil blending well with the cheese and sauce. For atmosphere, Verde is tough to beat.

Vinnie's Pizzeria, 148 Bedford Avenue, Williamsburg, (718) 782–7078. Open since 1960. Looks like a classic slice joint from the outside; not so inside. Veggie-oriented; no plain slices, at least this night; choices included zucchini and eggplant, sautéed spinach, broccoli, and pineapple (we'll forgive them for the last). Sign on wall: "Free Tibet with purchase of medium or large pizza." My black olive/mushroom/artichoke slice worked, despite an insubstantial crust. Would have liked to try a slice of the Great Grandma, but it was not available.

Manhattan

Abitino's Pizzeria, 1435 Broadway, (212) 768–0043. Mario and Anna Abitino emigrated to the United States from Naples in 1972, bringing their "secret family

Best pizzeria restroom sign ever. Abitino's Pizzeria, Manhattan.

recipes" with them. Mario worked in the pizza business for about twenty years before opening Abitino's in 1992. There's also an Abitino's at JFK. "Authentic New York pizza," reads a sign at the Broadway store. The fresh mozzarella slice features a perky tomato sauce; too bad the cheese is just average. You'll wish for more than two faint strips of sauce on the Grandma because the cheese—unattractively browned in spots—again lets the slice down. Abitino's does have my favorite pizzeria restroom sign in the city, though—"No Toilet Paper in Toilet; Use the Garbage"—written in no fewer than eight languages.

Adriana Pizzeria, 253 Third Avenue, (212) 674–6070. Decor includes the same neon-lit "Pizza 15¢" sidewalk stand photo you'll see in scores of pizzerias around the city; I really should have kept count. Norman Rockwell's iconic painting of a little boy and cop at the luncheonette is on the wall, and so is a takeoff on Edward Hopper's *Nighthawks*, with blue and yellow neon striping at top and bottom. The decor, as you can guess, is more noteworthy than the pizza. When the cheese takes on a grayish tinge, it's time to step away from the table. The sauce is no better.

Adrienne's Pizzabar, 54 Stone Street, (212) 248–3838. Stylish FiDi restaurant partly owned by Nick Angelis of Nick's Pizza in Forest Hills fame. Tables on cobblestoned Stone Street provide pizza al fresco. Inside the look is cool and casual, with votive-type lights at each table and a soothing late-night soundtrack. There may be no more topping-heavy pizza in the city; the burnt-edge "old-fashioned square," with crushed tomatoes and Parmesan cheese, is loaded with mushrooms and sausage, and quite good. The margherita, with the requisite San Marzano tomatoes, is solid if not spectacular.

Alberto's Pizza & Cheese Steak, 539 Sixth Avenue, (212) 989–0500. It's a "Famous Cheesesteak Factory" with some strangely worded pizza—the biancaneve features "snow white ricotta," and there are "Napoleon" and "Born to the Mexican" pizzas. You wouldn't expect to get a good slice at a cheesesteak joint, and you won't get one here. Slices are a buck, and that's about all they've got going for them. The faint peppery tinge lasts a second; the rest is mediocrity, highlighted by a soft, spongy crust. Noticeable gum line; take this slice to the pizza dentist.

Angelo's Pizza, 117 West 57th Street, (212) 333–4333. Attractive space—hardwood floors, drop ceiling, animated conversation. Whole pizzas only, plus pasta dishes. Where's the sauce? Right here; a half mushroom/half olive pizza downplays the cheese and gives sauce its say. Tasty, slightly charred crust, and the olives are kalamata; no messing around here. Solid pizza, though the tap beer selection is lame (Stella, Corona, and Bass, which tasted off).

Arome Deli and Pizza, 138 West 32nd Street, (212) 295–7870. Dollar slices come with a side of New York attitude. Sign on steps: "If you are not a customer you are not allowed up here." "Up here" is a dining room with hardwood floors; you may find Modelo tall-boys on the tables. Not sure if the cheese is real cheese or some synthetic stuff created in a lab somewhere. The crust is too bready-soft, but oregano comes somewhat to the rescue. At least it's a better slice than Rose's or Caruso's in Penn Station.

Artichoke, 328 East 14th Street, (212) 228–2004. Tiny takeout pie/slice joint with fifties music on the sound system, a lampshade made from a torn-stockinged

Don't even think about it. Arome Deli & Pizza, Manhattan.

Artichoke storefront, East 14th Street, Manhattan.

147

Sidewalk scene outside Artichoke, East 14th Street, Manhattan.

manikin's leg, one outside bench for sitting, and a stand-up-and-eat ledge not-so-romantically wedged against a chain-link fence. The margherita and Sicilian slices feature a nice tart sauce, but grated cheese atop the mozzarella tamps down the taste.

Arturo's Restaurant Pizzeria, 106 West Houston Street, (212) 677–3820. A series of cozy wood-paneled rooms with the requisite celeb photos; model airplanes hanging from the ceiling add a playful, creative touch. There's a grand piano in the corner for live jazz. When asked if the mushrooms were "special" or just "ordinary" mushrooms, the waitress answered "ordinary," so points for honesty. "Coal oven pizza" signs are everywhere. The mozzarella pizza—that's what it's called—is oily and buttery-crusted, but it's quite enjoyable. Fun place, but it can get crowded on weekends.

Bleecker Street Pizza, 69 Seventh Avenue South, (212) 924–4466. A fire engine pulls up, four NYC firemen walk in, pick up pizzas to go. Ten minutes later, two female traffic cops are at a table, eating slices. So are three foreign tourists. Bleecker Street Pizza has its share of celebrity customers—Alec Baldwin, Hugh Jackman,

Brooke Shields—and regular Joes and Janes attracted by the no-nonsense vibe and the supremely greasy, and good, plain slice. The Grandma slice is nowhere as good—weak tomato sauce, bland crust. Free refills on soda, and a curious beer selection that runs from Blue Moon to Matt's Southern Tier to Saigon.

Bravo Pizza, 6 East 42nd Street, (212) 867–4960. It looks touristy, or appears as just another Sbarro's knockoff near Grand Central Terminal, but this came as a nice surprise. They must love the color orange—orange neon, orange lettering, orange trays. The fresh mozzarella pizza is better than it has any right to be. The Sicilian is too bready/doughy and a bit undercooked, but the sauce saves it from mediocrity. The best pizza in this immediate neighborhood, although if you're in Grand Central itself, visit Two Boots.

Brick Oven Pizza 33, 268 23rd Street, (212) 206–0999. Located across the street from the wonderfully kitschy Trailer Park Lounge restaurant/bar, this pizzeria is a case of could-have-been. If the meat on the lasagna/chopped meat and mozzarella pizza had been fresher, this would be a standout. The ricotta is fresh and creamy, but the sauce simpers behind. The thin-crust Sicilian alla nonna with garlic—call it a Grandma—boasts a brighter, livelier sauce, and it's a success. We'll ignore the piece of chicken that somehow ended up on the lasagna pizza.

Caruso's, Penn Station, (212) 630–0350. "The largest slice in NYC," proclaims a sign in the window. Not even close: Koronet Pizza on the Upper West Side is twice the size. "The worst slice in Penn Station" is more like it. A pasty cornmeal-dusted crust and inferior cheese; it's a pizza for the desperate, and daredevil, among you.

Cavallo's Pizzeria, 324 Seventh Avenue, (212) 244–2012. Why is there so much mediocre pizza in and around Penn Station/Madison Square Garden? Add another to the list. There's a long buffet line of pizza choices; no matter what kind of pizza you like, you'll find it here. The plain slice, though, looks like it was run over by a passing bus. The Grandma, however, is better than its more celebrated counterpart at nearby Maffei; the cheese is brownish, but the sauce doesn't embarrass itself.

Celeste, 502 Amsterdam Avenue, (212) 874–4559. Brick-walled trattoria with skylit terrace, Italian-speaking staff, wood-burning oven, and dozens of pizza boxes discreetly stacked on a counter. Attentive service; a waiter promptly noticed my tilting table and quickly slid a piece of wood under the leg. Tasty sauce on the margherita pizza; just wish there were more of it.

Charlie's Pizza, 1501 Saint Nicholas Avenue, (212) 781–9089. Fluorescent-lit pizza dive with four tables, red-and-white tile floor. Sign: "Absolutely no credit," like it's a car dealership or something. A Fast and Furious sit-down video game is improbably wedged behind the pizza oven. The Sicilian packs a pleasant crunch, but the color of the pale yellow cheese matches the wall, which is never a good thing. The plain, with markedly better cheese than the Sicilian, is a good straightforward slice; you don't expect much on this stretch of the pizza highway, but it's a winner.

Cheesy Pizza, 2640 Broadway, (212) 662–5223. Gotta love the name; how could you resist a slice? "Taste it; you'll love it" is the slogan. Plenty of low-rent charm, with rickety tables, an eighties music soundtrack, and the revolving hypnotic action of a Slush Puppie machine. The plain slice seethes with grease and cheese; nothing

Charlie's Pizza, Manhattan.

special about this one. The margherita, though, works, with a pungent red sauce. In Cheesy Pizza, the sauce is better than the cheese.

Co., 230 Ninth Avenue, (212) 243–1105. Big doors (give them a good push) open to a wood-paneled space that may remind you of a Scandinavian pizzeria—or trippy airport lounge. Smallish bar; order or pick up takeout pizza there. Ignore the slightly pink tinge to the sauce on the margherita and take a bite; there's lots of chewy goodness there, with top-notch cheese and a more supple crust than most Neapolitans. There's a mere trace of sauce on the boscaiola, but the combination of onions, sausage, and mushrooms makes for a most holy taste trinity. It's a little sweet, a little spicy, and a lot of

149

satisfying. It's one of my twenty-five favorite pizzas in the city.

Donatella, 184 Eighth Avenue, (212) 493–5150. Odd moment before I even stepped inside; when I called in a takeout order, the manager asked for a credit card even though I insisted I would pay in cash. Uh, if you can't trust me to show up, why would I trust you with my credit card? I walked in and placed my order at the bar. Stylish restaurant, with marble-topped bar, yellow padded chairs, old-time street maps of Naples on the walls. Another unsliced pizza—like Franny's in Brooklyn—and it's nicely executed. For $10, it's a relative bargain considering the surroundings. The cappellaccio is a winning white pizza, with charred and marinated super-size mushrooms. A bit salty, but those are the mushrooms talking.

Don Pepe Pizza, Penn Station, (212) 967–4385. Online reviews proclaim this the best pizza in Penn Station. That's not saying much. Nothing looks particularly appetizing—unless your train is delayed and you're dying of hunger. It's a late-night, returning-from-a-Rangers-or-Knicks-game kind of slice; you don't want to wake up in the morning with this powdery-crusted, too-chewy pizza staring you in the face.

Eddie's Pizza Truck, various locations. You can get everything else in a NYC food truck, why not pizza? Sauce is spread on preformed dough, which is popped in an oven for about five minutes. The result? An extra-thin-crust pizza, crackly to the max. Stick to the plain cheese; the sausage is inferior. If you like truck food, you'll like it. I did. Pizza snobs will probably pass.

Empire Pizza II, 35 First Avenue, (212) 677–5500. Slices sit under individual mini heat lamps like movie stars at a tanning salon. Unfortunately they can't stand the spotlight. The cheese on the margherita looks like it's been soldered on. The plain slice is better, with more red sauce than the average New York slice. But the crust gives weak crust a bad name. There must be a napkin shortage; they keep them hidden behind the counter here.

Emporio, 231 Mott Street, (212) 966–1234. Cozy little tin-ceilinged hideout with brick walls, candles set atop ice, bottles of Peroni and La Rosa beer on a shelf. Eight tables along the wall, nine chairs at the bar, and plenty of room to move around. The margherita pizza is the thinnest of thin crusts, wispy but eminently tasty; the blackened crust flakes to cinders when you touch it. Could have used more sauce, though. Same owners of Aurora in Williamsburg and Aurora in SoHo.

Europan Pizza Cafe, 132 East 86th Street, (212) 828–2600. What's a "Europan"? It's a tiny, wood-floored cafe with cookies, paninis, spinach pies, lasagna—and pizza. The advertised Grandma is closer to a margherita, and in any case it's undermined by flimsy crust and foundation, despite acceptable sauce and cheese.

Famous Amadeus Pizza, 840 Eighth Avenue, (212) 489–6187. Across the street from Pizza Suprema, next to the Blarney Stone bar. A cheesy, unsurprising slice, but better than anything you'll find in nearby Penn Station. The Grandma, heavy on the garlic, looked promising but turned out piddling. The tomatoes could have been fresher. "Famous Amadeus" may rhyme, but the pizza's off-key.

Famous Ben's, 177 Spring Street, (212) 966–4494. Look for the pizza maker statue chained to the telephone pole out front. Six metal chairs on the sidewalk comprise the "sidewalk cafe," where thirty minutes is the "max" sitting time. Scene of a tabloid incident in the 1990s when bodyguards for Madonna roughed up photographer Ken Katz on the sidewalk; the *New York Post* article is proudly displayed in the window. Friendly staff; the girl behind the counter asks if I want a corner or middle of their "famous square" pizza. It's nice and chewy, unlike the spongy bread of Pizza Suprema's Sicilian. Other choices include round slices, a square marinara, and a Palermo with onion sauce and bread crumbs. The restroom key is attached to a massive bolt that would stun a horse.

Sign for sidewalk cafe, such as it is, outside Famous Ben's in Manhattan.

Famous Original Ray's Pizza, 204 Ninth Avenue, (212) 243–1129. One of nine Famous Ray's outposts owned by the Mangano family. There's a stand-up counter up front and big dining room out back; with the large-screen TV, you could turn it into your favorite Sunday afternoon football-watching pizza spot. The plain slice's best quality is its thick, chewy crust. There's all sorts of bad pizzeria art out there; the murals on the walls here are one-of-a-kind mosaic-tiled scenes of Venice.

Farinella Italian Bakery Pizza, 1132 Lexington Avenue, (212) 327–2702. Cozy little pizza cafe in a neighborhood starving for late-night pizzerias. The boxes, highlighted by a grinning straw-hatted man who looks more carnival barker than pizza maker, are Manhattan's coolest. Two slices cost $9, but each is cut into two moderate-sized ones. The margherita comes off better than the mushroom—sorry, the funghi—but the cheese on both tasted a bit pasty. One novelty: the four-foot-long, rectangular palam pizzas.

Fat Sal's Pizza, 510 Ninth Avenue, (212) 594–9462. Two tables, four chairs, white-tiled wall. Fat Sal's serves fat slices, and they're good ones. The cheese pizza features a pleasant little basil boost; it may be the best plain slice in this neighborhood. Good job on the margherita—you won't be embarrassed to be seen in public with it. There are five Fat Sal's locations in all—here, plus Tenth Avenue, West 14th Street, Avenue A, and Second Avenue.

Box for Fat Sal's, Manhattan.

FDR 99¢ Pizza, 150 East 2nd Street, (212) 253–5950. There's no connection to the twenty-third president of the United States for this place, as far as I know. No tables or seats, but there's a long stand-up counter where you can add spices to liven up your universally bland dollar slice. Or you can do what I did and take your slice outside and place it on the covered garbage cans on the sidewalk. Kindly woman behind counter hands out slices one by one from the Baker's Pride oven. Decent cheese, and squarely in the middle of the pack as far as dollar slices; if the crust had any crisp, they'd have something.

Goodfellas Old World Brick Oven Pizza & Pasta, 144 Orchard Street, (212) 432–3200. International Pizza Expo's "World's Best Pizza"—three times! Well, the Old World Style pizza, a margherita, is better than most. No fireworks, just a good, honest—and slightly boring— pizza. There's also a four-cheese pizza with mozzarella, provolone, fontina, and grated pecorino, and for those who must have chicken on their pizza, a Sally Pie with lemon garlic chicken, roasted rosemary potatoes, cheddar cheese, and mushrooms, topped with a "gourmet" cheddar scallion cream sauce. You try it; I won't.

Gotham Pizza, 144 Ninth Avenue, (212) 989–8858. Spacious, brick-walled, mom-and-kids kind of pizza

Box, Gotham Pizza, Ninth Avenue, Manhattan.

joint. Guy behind counter takes orders in rapid fire; be ready. The plain is a nice slice, liberally seasoned, with a pleasant crisp and crunch when you bite into it. The Grandma gets good marks for seasoning, demerits for its runny oily pools on top.

Grandpa's Brick Oven Pizza, 4973 Broadway, (212) 304–1185. You can't go much farther north in Manhattan for pizza. Absolutely the coolest Christmas decorations of any pizzeria in the city—an opening and closing mailbox, two reindeer in a hot air balloon, white reindeer with a rotating head (try to get those Linda Blair fantasies out of your mind), green and red gift boxes. Oh, the pizza. The plain is true thin-crust, and a good one, cheesy and crispy. The Sicilian, alas, is unfortunate, with unpleasant faded brown cheese on top.

Gray's Papaya, 402 Sixth Avenue, (212) 260–3532. About the last place you'd expect to find a decent dollar slice is this juice/hot dog landmark. But it's better than average. Note I said dollar slice; it's still a long way from the regular slice at, say, Bleecker Street Pizza, several blocks away. The slice is nice and oily, with a substantial crust, but the cheese teeters on tastelessness. Fun late-night hangout, with the multicolored paper pineapples, oranges, and grapes dangling from the ceiling like a Busby Berkeley production number run amok.

Harry's Italian Pizza Bar, 2 Gold Street, (212) 747–0797. With its communal tables, TV screens, and lively crowd, it may remind you more of a sports bar than an upscale pizzeria. "No slices!" the menu proclaims. Same owners as Adrienne's Pizzabar, also in FiDi. The white pizza here is crispier and a bit more charred than the square. The sausage is not as good, or at least didn't taste as good, as Adrienne's. My dining companion preferred Harry's over Adrienne's: I was the opposite. There are sister locations at Rockefeller Center and Battery Park City.

Hell's Kitchen Pizza, 691 Tenth Avenue, (212) 765–8565. Pizza with a difference, and not just because of the painted flames licking the walls. Red-checked tablecloths; are there red-checked tablecloths even in hell? Owner Sajid Alam took over ownership in 2011 and added his own seasoning spin; the Hellfire pizza scorches with what he calls "seven country spice mix," with spices from Jamaica, Mexico, India, and elsewhere bringing the heat. The Hellfire, with mozzarella, hot Italian sausage, pepperoni, and cherry peppers, may be the city's spiciest slice. It's overly greasy but thoroughly enjoyable. The Grandma or Sicilian—Alam calls it both—boasts a tangy sauce but ordinary cheese.

Menu board at Hell's Kitchen Pizza, Manhattan.

Iggy's Pizzeria, 173 First Avenue, (212) 353–3331. A Grandma-pizza-shaped, tin-ceilinged space with photos of Italian street scenes on the walls and a large blue peace sign against a white background. On pizzeria

decor alone, it gets high marks. The plain slice is a pleasant little number, with oil running down ridges like a fast-flowing pizza river. The square marinara boasts an aggressive, tart tomato sauce that's better than 95 percent of the red stuff out there. The crust is too buttery-tasting, but I'm not complaining—much.

Joe's Pizza, 7 Carmine Street, (212) 366–1182. Another NYC pizza legend, Joe's started at the corner of Carmine and Bleecker in 1975, moving to its current location, just down the block, in 2005. Owner Joe Pozzuoli, nearing eighty, still makes deliveries in his car. There's exactly one table, but several ledges for stand-up dining. You can almost always count on getting a fresh slice; the 600-degree oven cooks pizza in five minutes, and traffic is constant. It's a classic New York slice, thinner and crispier than most, oozing oily goodness. You want garlic knots or calzones? Go elsewhere.

John's, 260 West 44th Street, (212) 391–7560. You're unsure whether you're walking into a pizzeria, sports bar (high-def TVs, lively crowd), or club, with a pulsing dance beat. What you're definitely in is a former church; check out the dome and stained-glass windows. Drinks and pizza come with a free side of NYC bartender attitude. "You gotta eat this pizza hot," the one on duty told me. "Don't take it home." Guess I looked like a tourist—or someone who had never eaten pizza in his life. In any event, it's good pizza, thinner than most, nice and saucy, neither too crispy or too chewy. Don't you dare take it home!

John's on Bleecker, 278 Bleecker Street, (212) 243–1680. Legendary Village pizzeria opened by John Sasso, who honed his craft at Lombardi's, in 1929. Bring your Swiss Army knife and carve your initials or favorite sayings on the walls, like thousands before you. There are no fewer than fifty-four pizzas—just varying combinations of sauce, cheese, meat, and veggies—on the menu; if the fine type makes you dizzy, just tell the waitress what you want on your pizza. A half plain/half sausage is commendable—good chunk sausage and a puffy, chewy, slightly charred crust, although it might have benefited by a bit more crisp. Avoid Sundays; they're the busiest day here.

Keste, 271 Bleecker Street, (212) 243–1500. Friendly staff; they encouraged us to move from the table squeezed next to the front door to one in the center of the small, narrow, hardwood-floored dining room. Photos of a wistful-looking child with a pizza in front of him and of a flour-covered hand holding a ball of mozzarella add to the homey atmosphere. There's animated conversation and hip-hop music in the background; don't go expecting a quiet romantic dinner. A prosciutto de Parma pizza brought exclamations from my pizza pal, Kristin. "The best basil I've ever had," she said. The crust seems a bit too chewy, though. The tomatoes atop the regina margherita are uber-fresh, but the pizza seemed a bit undercooked. A must-stop, at any rate, on the Neapolitan-pizza-sampling circuit. "Buona sera," the manager says cheerily as we leave.

K Food Corp., 18 East 33rd Street, (212) 213–5100. The only dollar-slice pizzeria in the city to offer Himalayan pink crystal salt—the only pizzeria, period. "Provides numerous health benefits and it enhances the food's flavor," according to a sign on the wall. The makers of the Original Himalayan Crystal Salt say the salt is "pure" and "unpolluted" and comes "from a time when the Earth was pristine." The salt "is waiting for its moment to have its inherent stored energy, its bio-

energetic content set free by combining it with water." What effect does all this have on K Food's dollar slice? Nothing, as far as I can tell. Weak crust and brownish cheese, but there's a pleasing little crunch underneath. Plunk down a couple extra bucks and get the veggie slice, loaded with tomatoes, mushrooms, black olives, peppers, red onions, and spinach. There are more photos of tomatoes on the wall than in any other pizzeria in the city. Trust me, I've been keeping track.

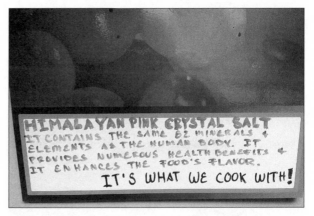

K Food Corp., Manhattan, the only pizzeria to use Himalayan pink crystal salt.

Koronet Pizza, 2848 Broadway, (212) 222–1566. Forget about other pizzerias claiming "the biggest slice" in the city. Koronet offers a monster—ninety square inches by one estimation. It's bigger than your head; it may be bigger than your two-year-old. Tile floors, just three tables, a dozen stools and shelf along one wall, four stools along another. The plain is a mondo-cheesy slice, agreeably oily, and a relative bargain at $3.75. Nothing special taste-wise, but for circus-geek factor, it's a must. Message on restroom wall: "While you're taking a s——, make sure to follow me on Twitter."

Krust Pizzeria, 226 East 14th Street, (212) 510–8869. Tiny red-shuttered storefront, with six stools, yellow walls, and the two TVs tuned to a soccer game. The plain is more margherita than a classic New York slice, and rather ordinary. The crust is nothing special; they may want to reconsider the name.

Krust Pizzeria, East 14th Street, Manhattan.

La Pizzeria, 442 Third Avenue, (212) 532–0097. Name like that, you'd better be good. Handsome space—wood paneling, mirrored walls, neon-lit. The "thin-crust mozzarella" pizza has a barely cooked crust and generic tomatoes. Lofty name, lackluster pizza.

L'asso, 192 Mott Street, (212) 219–2353. You'll often find co-owner Greg Barris, a stand-up comedian, in here, eating lunch or sampling a new dessert. They use organic tomato sauce and nonbromated flour (bromated flour, used by most pizzerias, can cause long-term negative health effects, according to Barris). Pizzas include the San Daniele (tomato sauce, mozzarella, arugula, prosciutto, Parmesan, and extra-virgin olive oil), albondiga (sauce, mozzarella, homemade meatballs, onions, and fresh garlic), and Roma (walnut pesto, mozzarella, and rosemary). The Big D, with tomato sauce, bufala and regular mozzarella, shaved pecorino, and basil, is big on flavor, charred-crusted, and not as drippy as bufala mozzarella pizzas can be. There's another location at 107 First Avenue.

Lazzara's Pizza Cafe & Restaurant, 221 West 38th Street, (212) 944–7792. Walk up the steep subway-steps-like entrance to the formidable front door, then another flight of stairs, and bear right into the dining room, a cozy retreat from the Times Square tumult. Soul music tastefully plays in the background. Tony and Sebastian Lazzara opened Lazzara's in 1985; there is another location on Ninth Avenue. "New York's Best Thin Crust Pizza," proclaims the menu. Not quite. The toppings on the Lazzara's Special—prosciutto, sun-dried tomatoes, and olives—are fine, but the sauce is nondescript. Waitress, watching a marathon on TV: "My boyfriend ran in high school. Now he is fat."

Libretto's Pizzeria, 546 Third Avenue, (212) 213–6445. Sign in window proclaims it's on somebody-or-other's best-pizza-in-New-York list. Takeout counter up front, spacious brick-walled dining room in back; high-def TVs give it a sports bar feel. The plain is on a par with the standard Third Avenue slice; a mushroom slice comes off better. Guy in corner to girlfriend: "I'm a pretty cool cat, but when I see someone hitting on you . . ."

Lil' Frankie's, 19 First Avenue, (212) 420–4900. Frank Prisinzano opened his thirty-two-seat pizzeria in January 2002, adding a glass-enclosed back patio and fifty more seats five months later. The following year, he launched East Village Radio, a community radio station that streams from a street-level studio on First Avenue. The Big Cheech Bar, named after the nickname of Prisinzano's father, is a cozy nook made for lazy after-noons. The wood-burning brick oven features "real lava" from Vesuvio, as if that were something special. The pizza, in any case, is excellent. If only every mushroom pizza tasted like the Pizza Funghi here, with fat little mushrooms, a fresh-tasting sauce, and lightly burnt crust. The Pizza Salsiccia boasts super sausage; wish there were more of it. The olive oil pools pleasingly amidst the vine-ripe tomatoes and mozzarella. Lil' Frankie's is on my list of the ten most fun pizzerias in the city.

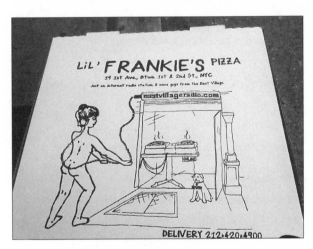

Groovy box, Lil' Frankie's, Manhattan.

Little Italy Pizza, 2 East 33rd Street, (212) 481–5200. I should have kept track of all the pizzerias with the word "famous" on their window or menus; here's another one. Popular moms-and-kids spot, apparently;

the place looked like grade school recess. The plain slice is kind of gummy—you'll do better with a slice at the dollar joints. The fresh mozzarella/red sauce pizza is markedly better, with a seriously thick coating of cheese and a decent sauce. I'd use it for a meatball sandwich more than pizza. "You're supposed to be cuter than me," one eight-year-old says to her older sister. "It doesn't matter who's cuter," Mom weighs in immediately. "I love you both."

Lombardi's, 32 Spring Street, (212) 941–7994. In 1905, Gennaro Lombardi received a license to sell pizza from the city of New York, becoming the country's first pizzeria. It was a training ground for soon-to-be-pizza legends; John Sasso of John's on Bleecker, Anthony Pero of Totonno's, and Pasquale "Patsy" Lancieri of Patsy's would all start at Lombardi's. Lombardi's is no quaint old-school pizzeria; the dining rooms are spacious, and perpetually packed. But the menu has changed only slightly over the years; there are no Sicilian, Grandma, chicken, or specialty pizzas on the menu, just the "original" pizza with fifteen toppings available, and a white pizza. An original, with mozzarella and a San Marzano tomato sauce and topped with Romano and basil, is satisfying in a simple, straightforward way.

Luigi's Restaurant, 304 Eighth Avenue, (212) 242–2259. Redbrick wall, five booths, tiny TV tuned to Italian programming. The bathroom is one of

Luigi's, Eighth Avenue, Manhattan.

the city's least glamorous, with heavily graffitied walls. The cash register and phone are both wrapped in plastic—are they expecting radioactive flour fallout? The plain slice offers a slightly sweet sauce, but the cheese is nearly tasteless. Same with the extremely bready Sicilian; it tastes like they wrapped a protective layer around it to keep out all taste and flavor.

Luna Pizzeria, 225 Park Row, (212) 385–8118. Affable owner scrambles for a pen to add up the bill. "When I was in the fish business and there was a bill due," he says, "you'd say, 'I lost my pen.'" Former Baby-O Brick Oven Pizzeria, now a cheery little cafe with Italian drink posters on the walls. The margherita is nothing special, but there's good sauce and cheese, and there's something to be said for solid. The Sicilian is similarly well built, but there's an unfortunate uncooked-dough line between cheese and bread.

Luzzo's, 211–213 First Avenue, (212) 473–7447. Handsome pizza hangout, with brick walls, hardwood floors, and a window frame and upside-down table and chair playfully hanging from the tin ceiling. One of the few coal-burning ovens in the city; they also use wood. Neapolitan-style pizzas, although owner Michele Iuliano doesn't exactly play by the strict Neapolitan rules; for example, there's sugar in the dough, a big Neapolitan no-no. Lombardi's was stop one and Luzzo's stop two on one of Scott Wiener's Pizza Tours; I thought Luzzo's crust topped Lombardi's, but the Luzzo's sauce seemed a bit off-putting. Made New York magazine's Top Twenty Pies of the Moment list.

Maffei Pizza, 668 Sixth Avenue, (212) 929–0949. Warm, welcoming red/green neon sign, but it goes downhill from there. Heralded on pizza blogs for its

Grandma slice, but this is one Grandma you don't want in your pizza family. It's too greasy, too gooey, too buttery, too much of all the wrong things. The plain slice is king-sized and decent, despite ancient-looking cheese. At two bucks, it's at least three times better than the dollar slices in the neighborhood.

Mamani Pizza, 151 Avenue A, (212) 388–1715. "Persian home style wraps and falafel" meet dollar slices at this tiny neighborhood spot. No tables, just four stools and a ledge. The menu includes white meat popcorn chicken, corn dogs, egg rolls, and Philly cheesesteaks. Regular pizzas include a Mexican fiesta veggie pizza, a Greek-style veggie pizza, and a "cheeseless" pizza. Call the plain dollar slice bread with sauce. Don't tilt it; everything will slide right off onto the floor or onto your lap. That being said, a hot slice is hardly unpleasant: I wouldn't kick that red sauce out of my kitchen.

Merilu Pizza al Metro, 791 Ninth Avenue, (212) 541–5012. No-frills pizzeria with just four tables and, on a Saturday night, just three kinds of pizza. Mushrooms slightly above average; the standout here is the sweetish red sauce. Slices are $4, but they're big. The lineup includes Italian Vegetariana, a Rustica, and Lou's Spicy Buffalo Chicken. Cozy, quiet little spot amidst the bright lights of Ninth Avenue.

Mike's Pizza, 132 East 23rd Street, (212) 473–8900. A Gray's Papaya knockoff, with the requisite papaya, banana, mango, and piña colada drinks inside one entrance and dollar-slice pizza next door. They should do something about the pizza on the takeout menu; it doesn't look very appetizing. Infinitesimally thicker—or is that less thin?—than the average dollar slice, with a funky, slightly peppery flavor that could have been all

wrong but turns out all right. House soundtrack is eighties pop/rock.

Mimi's Pizza & Restaurant, 1248 Lexington Avenue, (212) 861–3363. An Upper East Side pizza legend. Dig the Beatles poster on the wall signed by Sid Bernstein, producer of the Beatles Shea Stadium concert in 1965. Tickets were $4.50, $5, and $5.75. Takeout counter and several tables to the left, a homey little dining room to the right. The plain slice is crazy-cheesy and agreeably salty. The Sicilian, though, is a loser; the cheese peels right off the top, and even a first-time pizza eater knows it's not supposed to do that.

Motorino, 349 East 12th Street, (212) 777–2644. Those who despaired when Mathieu Palombino's Williamsburg location closed when the building collapsed need only hop the subway to his East Village outpost. The Belgium-born chef uses primo ingredients and loves his oven; he acquired the space, and the $15,000 wood-burning Acunto oven inside, from Anthony Mangieri, owner of the former, highly acclaimed Una Pizza Napoletana. Inside the tiny restroom is the lyric sheet to "That's Amore." You may fall in love with the margherita pizza, a relative bargain at $9 considering the quality of ingredients. It's highlighted with a sweet, near-sensational sauce and a blackened crust that flakes off like cinders in a campfire. The meaty/spicy/oily combination on the sopressata picante pizza is devastating. The *New York Times*'s Sam Sifton has called it the city's best pizza. In my opinion, there are a handful of contenders.

Naked Pizza, 954 Third Avenue, (212) 759–3500. One look at the menu and your eyes can glaze over, with the build-your-own-pizza approach and talk of prebiotic agave fiber, amaranth, teff, and spelt. "We intend to

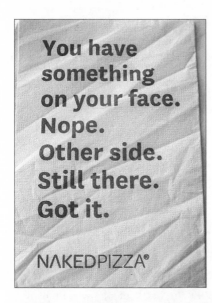

Napkin with a message, Naked Pizza, Manhattan.

Naked Pizza, Third Avenue, Manhattan.

launch the world's largest grassroots movement," says co-founder Jeff Leach, who started Naked Pizza in a flooded-out New Orleans bakery. The idea is all-natural ingredients, with ten-grain dough and no sugar or hydrogenated oil added. The sausage boasts an agreeable smoky flavor, but the sauce makes little impression even though it's supposed to be "nicely spiced and herbed." Toppings run from fresh basil, cilantro, and artichokes to black beans, fire-roasted peppers, and spinach.

99¢ Fresh Pizza, 569 Ninth Avenue, (212) 268–1461. This sidewalk stand in the shadow of the Port Authority Bus Terminal has a late-night Edward Hopper feel, with bright fluorescent lighting, stark signage, and a grungy charm, making it look like a relic of 42nd Street before it was cleaned up. The plain cheese slice is a bit rubbery but somehow not unpleasant (neat trick, that). The sausage is spicy, but that's the only thing going for it. 2 Bros. does a better dollar slice, but 99¢ Fresh Pizza is an improvement over the sorry mess that passes for pizza inside the bus terminal.

99¢ Pizza, East 44th Street and Third Avenue. Not connected to 99¢ Fresh Pizza, one of whose locations is

Sign outside Naked Pizza on East 14th Street, Manhattan.

two blocks away, on East 43rd Street just off Third Avenue. 99¢ Pizza is a tiny white-walled space with barely enough room for two or three people to maneuver in. The crust is one of the worst in the dollar-slice world: too soft, too chewy, undercooked. Three strikes and you're out.

Numero 28 Pizzeria, 196 Spring Street, (212) 219–9020. The only one of three Numero 28 locations to offer slices, with creative styles, toppings, and combinations and nary a chicken pizza in sight. The crostini al prosciutto will tempt those wishing to go meatless and tomatoless; the buttery, oily shell and cheesy/meaty mix make for a fine, filling slice. The mozzarella atop the bufala pizza looks like it's been glued on—there's practically no give—but it's a satisfying slice, with a distinctive pebbly foundation and juicy cherry tomatoes on top.

Off Broadway Deli & Pizza, 726 Eighth Avenue, (212) 398–3981. Papa John's dollar slice boasts the biggest crust in its field; Off Broadway has the biggest slice, period. It's far from Koronet Pizza size, but it's ample, and almost tasty, with a little oregano and other seasoning. The crust has the familiar cheap mushy texture, but there's a faint crispiness underneath, which for a dollar slice is practically front-page news. "Where foods are made fresh" is the slogan at this deli/pizzeria, which offers everything from pancakes, falafel, panini, and wraps to spaghetti and meatballs, sliced steak, and linzer tarts. Here's why you attend this Off Broadway show—the upstairs "private" dining room. It's not fancy (pale green walls), but it's big (several dozen tables) and has Internet terminals. Late afternoon, you may have the room entirely to yourself, as I did.

Olympia Gourmet Deli, 761 Sixth Avenue, (212) 924–5074. Delis have joined the dollar-slice craze—so far with regrettable results. Stick to corn muffins, wraps, and chicken sandwiches, please. The plain slice is crispier and heftier than most, but the crust is softer than a pillow, and I'd rather eat a pillow.

Otto, One Fifth Avenue, (212) 995–9559. Located in the historic Art Deco One Fifth Avenue building, Otto is one of a dozen restaurants in New York, Las Vegas, and Los Angeles owned by Mario Batali and Joe Bastianich. The always-packed front bar and wood-paneled dining room combine, according to its owners, the "elegance of an Italian enoteca with the fun bustle of a crowded Italian train station." Pasta and pizzas are reasonably priced, considering the surroundings and the owners' star power. The vongole (clam) pizza sure is pretty to look at it—a mini mountain of baby clams in shells atop a mozzarella/garlic-topped pizza. But why force the diner to scoop out the tiny clams one by one and spread them over the cheese? Or are they not supposed to be? Taste-wise, it doesn't add up to much anyway. The cacio e pepe (mozzarella, cacio cheese, pecorino, Parmigiano, black pepper) pizza is markedly better.

Papa John's, 213 West 28th Street, (212) 563–7272. One of four Papa John's in the city with dollar slices; at the West Side location, they're available from 10:30 A.M. to 6:30 P.M. Monday through Friday only. And they're not a dollar. Unlike most other dollar-slice joints, Papa John's charges you tax, which means a slice will set you back $1.08. Which makes you wonder why Papa John's doesn't just charge 93 cents, the tax making it an even dollar; it would also keep employees from handing out a ton of change each time. Anyway, it's the city's thickest dollar slice, with the familiar Papa John's taste. The crust is too soft but somehow pleasantly chewy. The cheese is blah. The interior of the restaurant resembles a bus station waiting room more than a pizzeria: yellow walls, eight tables. Love the fire escape ladder dangling over the outside sign.

Park Row Deli & Pizza/Park Row Eatery, 38 Park Row, (212) 962–2833. Green mirrored walls with a table filled with magazines (*Allure, Smithsonian, Vogue,* etc.), like a pizzeria version of the dentist's office. The plain is good and oily, with a nice little crisp underneath, but it's let down by a mushy, insubstantial crust.

Pastafina, 388 Third Avenue, (212) 251–0708. Several interesting choices, including a white pizza with mushrooms and olives. The Sicilian is thicker than a phonebook; it could double as a doorstop. Great gobs of tomatoes on the marinara, but the basil is tired-looking and the crust bland. If the sausage, green peppers, and red onions slice weren't so oily/greasy, it would be edible.

Patsy's, 2287 First Avenue, East Harlem, (212) 534–9783. Immigrant newlyweds Pasquale "Patsy" and Carmella Lancieri opened their East Harlem pizzeria in 1933. Patsy, like John Sasso of John's and Anthony Pero of Totonno's, learned his craft at Lombardi's on Spring Street. In the 1970s, Francis Ford Coppola, working on *The Godfather,* took Al Pacino to Patsy's; the restaurant was the inspiration for Michael Corleone's shooting of mobster Sollozzo and police captain McCluskey in the movie. You can get slices three doors down from the main entrance to the restaurant. The plain comes off as a disappointment; it's not the slice's floppiness or flimsiness, it's just the cheese, average at best. Good sweet sauce, although it's barely there.

Piazza 17, 17 Cleveland Place, (212) 334–6534. Next to Eileen's Special Cheesecake, it's practically hidden; you may walk right past it. Handsome space—in the former Club Veloce—with brick walls, floor-to-ceiling menu board, twenty tables, De Cecco pasta on the shelves. Every once in a while, there was an unexpected surprise in my pizza sampling; Piazza 17 was one of them. The square marinara, with grated cheese on top and a nice mellow sauce, is first-rate. A slice with mushrooms and black olives is similarly satisfying; anyone who uses kalamatas instead of regular black olives cares. Intriguing choices: the Bella (mozzarella, tomatoes, prosciutto, eggplant) and Rustica (sausage, mozzarella, gorgonzola, tomatoes), among others.

Pizza Box, 176 Bleecker Street, (212) 979–0823. You gotta love the name, but the most pleasant surprise is walking through the sterile pizza-boothed dining room and finding a pleasant tree-shaded outdoor patio. You don't see many Grandma pizzas in this neighborhood, but Pizza Box makes a saucy, oregano-laced one, though you may wish the sauce were spryer. For just $2, though, it's good value. Beer is on tap, and there are various Pizza Box Beer and Wine Combos available.

Pizza by Certe, 132 East 56th Street, (212) 813–2020. The tumble of plants on the wall is not for show—herbs are picked from there and added to the food, which includes sandwiches, entrees, and handmade pasta. Emphasis on fresh and local; the flour is never bleached or bromated, and no canned tomatoes are used. Slices are served on bamboo plates. Does it all add up to good pizza? I loved the description of the Godfather—"a chiffonade of cured salumeria meats"—and while the

Pizza Box, Bleecker Street, Manhattan.

margherita is runny but tasty, the crust nice and chewy. Other choices: Patata (whole wheat crust, potato, mozzarella, Parmigiano, thyme) and Forestiera (rosemary ham, mushrooms, ricotta, mozzarella).

Pizza Gaga, 171 West 23rd Street, (212) 647–8777. No connection to Lady-you-know-who. Located right outside the 23rd Street 1 and 2 subway stop; the windowsill makes for a prime people-watching spot. Free soda with the purchase of two slices. The plain slice is painfully boring, but the margherita, with fresh

result is greasy, it's a nice muscular alternative to pepperoni and the like. The bianco combines a delicate dash of truffle oil, arugula, pepper, and a ricotta you could fall in love with.

Pizza by La Girolla, 403 Amsterdam Avenue, (212) 721–0900. About a dozen kinds of slices are available, or you can assemble one like a car, with broccolini, sopressata, tuna in olive oil, pine nuts, and porcini dust among the toppings. There are whole round and rectangular pizzas, six-inch rounds, and slices. The most popular topping is artichoke. The sauce on the

Pizza Gaga, West 23rd Street, Manhattan.

Kristin Federico at Pizza Gaga, Manhattan.

distinctive quality, even more than the ton of garlic, is its funky-tasting red sauce. The plain slice has just about the strangest-tasting cheese anywhere—not bad-strange, just odd, leaving you wondering what kind of cheese it is, exactly. I'll give them this much—they had the only free calendars of any pizzeria visited.

Pizza Plus, 707 Ninth Avenue, (212) 245–6260. Can you trust a pizzeria that also promises "the best cheese-steak in New York"? Attractive, brick-walled space with backlit floral design panels. Surprisingly good plain slice,

basil and a tart little sauce, will have you dancing. That's the first, and last, Lady-you-know-who song reference.

Pizza Haven, 4942 Broadway, (212) 569–3720. "You ring, we bring" is the motto at this fluorescent-lit pizza dive. Gotta love any place that offers "hippie rolls"—calzones with sausage, peppers, and mozzarella. They don't explain the "hippie" part. The focaccia slice's most

"You Ring, We Bring," Pizza Haven, Manhattan.

Pizza Haven, Broadway, Manhattan.

163

with a good crisp. Formulaic crust, but the oily cheesy goodness on top tips the scales. The margherita, with a blackened crust, is right out of Dullsville. Sign in window: "Your truly am and pm people," whatever that means.

Pizza Pub, 294 Third Avenue, (212) 477–8100. Pizza Pub? Why didn't someone think of this before? Bar in front, pizza counter and oven in back. Stylish in a frat house kind of way—red walls, faux moosehead, cozy red banquettes by the window. The Sicilian is a nearly all-white pizza done as a square, and it's nearly good. Distinct crispiness, but the crust is too oily. The five-cheese pizza (mozzarella, Gorgonzola, Romano, goat, and asiago) fairly shimmers with oil, but it's a decent bar slice. The Sicilian grew on me, though, and it had nothing to do with the bottle of Little Sumpin' Ale consumed.

PizzArte, 69 West 55th Street, (212) 247–3936. Probably the city's most striking pizzeria space; the walls in the two-floor restaurant are decorated with artwork from Italian artists. Bar downstairs, tables on both floors. The two pizzas sampled both seemed too doughy and chewy, but the prosciutto on the pulcinella pizza (also with mozzarella, cherry tomatoes, arugula, and shaved Parmigiano) is first-rate. Pizzas include the Verace (San Marzano tomatoes, bufala mozzarella, basil), the PizzArte (zucchini, speck, burrata), and the fried-then-baked Montanara pizza.

Pizza Roma, 259 Bleecker Street, (212) 924–1970. One of the newer additions to the already-crowded Bleecker Street pizza scene, Roma, housed in the former Zito's Bakery, tries to distance itself from the pack with high-end ingredients—and higher prices. Slices run from $3 to $6. If you like mushrooms, a porcini slice here is

close to heaven. Other choices include Tartufina (with truffle and fontina cheese) and boscaiola (sausage and porcini, no cheese). Make sure your slice is hot; they rushed mine out of the oven.

Pizza Suprema, 413 Eighth Avenue, (212) 594–8939. Brightly-lit pizzeria (don't come here if you have a hangover; it'll hurt) "owned by the same Italian family" since 1964. "Here before MSG," reads another sign, a reference to the World's Most Famous Arena. When owner Salvatore Riggio raised the price of a slice in the 1960s, students from a nearby school picketed out front. A cult favorite, and the best pizza in or around Madison Square Garden/Penn Station. They use four different sauces on the pizza, which may be some kind of record. Good plain slice; fat, too-chewy Sicilian. The upside-down slice is better than either, with its uber-crunchy and hard-baked crust, but the bread is kind of blah.

Pomodoro Pizza, 166 Second Avenue, (212) 982–8880. An attempt at quasi-authenticity, with varying-sized bottles of Pellegrino on one shelf, imported cookies on another. "We deliver fine wine and hard liquor," the menu promises. Dig the Astroturf-like carpet on the outside patio. The plain pizza is far from authentic, but it's decent. The white is, as they say in New York, from hunger, with its anemic, not-fully-cooked splotches of ricotta.

Pop's Dollar Food Shop/Spinelli's Pizza/Gyro II, 427 Seventh Avenue, (212) 212–2000. Weird but fun food court straight from Long Island or Jersey, and shrunk down to size. Pop's and the dollar-food menu— pizza, burgers, hot dogs—is located in the back, but the day I visited, dollar slices were being sold at the Spinelli's counter up front. The slice is thin, floppy, and

A chart on Ray's wall broke down all your favorite pizzas.

One last slice at Ray's on Prince Street.

October 30, 2011
will be our
last day of
business.

Thank you for your patronage.
We will miss you all.

Ray's
RESTAURANT
AND PIZZERIA

Sign outside Ray's, which closed in October 2011.

eminently forgettable. If you remember it for anything, it's because they do something almost unheard-of in the dollar-slice world: they charge you tax, which makes your dollar slice $1.09. Which makes it a penny more than its counterpart at Papa John's, in case you're on a seriously tight budget.

Ray's Pizza, 27 Prince Street. This legendary Nolita pizzeria closed October 20, 2011, due to "increased rent," according to a sign posted in the window, although word is that it will reopen elsewhere. Wood-slatted benches and a plain slice with personality—splotches of pleasingly burnt cheese; soft, chewy crust. RIP Ray's—hope you return.

Ray's Pizza Bagel Cafe, 2 St. Marks Place, (212) 533–6656. A buffet line of pizza, calzone, muffins, bagels; tables on the sidewalk and a decent beer selection. Grated cheese atop the margherita is overkill; the mozzarella can stand on its own, thank you. If you like oregano, this is your place; the plain slice is blanketed with it. If you want to go cheaper and better, 2 Bros. is right down the street.

Rivoli Pizza, 176 Seventh Avenue South, (212) 691–2704. "Taste the difference" is the slogan at this attractive green-and-red-walled, hardwood-floored space; it looks more like a Mexican cantina than an Italian pizzeria. The white pizza offers big splotches of ricotta, but the feeble crust tastes like it never got out of kindergarten. At least it's better than the Sicilian; the off-putting cheese tastes like it came from another dairy planet.

Rocky's Brick Oven Pizzeria & Restaurant, 304 West 14th Street, (212) 242–2345. Cute little place, with four tables and five stools along a wall decorated with photos of Brando, De Niro, and Stallone, plus a pair of red Everlast boxing gloves atop the fax machine. Just steps from the 14th Street A, C, E subway stop. There's a pleasant peppery, smoky tinge to the plain pizza, although the crust is commonplace. An all-mushroom slice features above-average 'shrooms, but it's ordinary otherwise.

Roll n Go, 362 Broadway, (212) 925–7655. A roll, presumably, to go—OK, I get it—but it sounds more like the instructions for what you're supposed to do when you're on fire. If there's one constant among dollar slices, it's the chewy undercooked crust. Memo to all dollar-slice operators: cook the pizza longer, you'll get more customers. The *Village Voice*'s Robert Sietsema called Roll n Go's teriyaki slice one of the city's five worst slices, period. The plain slice here is only slightly better than the ones at 99¢ Pizza and Olympia Gourmet Deli, but that's not saying much. The only thing going for Roll n Go: it's the closest dollar-slice joint to the World Trade Center PATH station.

Rosario's Pizza, 173 Orchard Street, (212) 777–9813. Walk-up window, six tables inside, and a sign that reads, "Don't kiss the chef." The Rustica pizzas here feature thick, formidable crusts; the Rustica Alla Campagnola joins sausage, pepperoni, peppers, and cheese. There's a burger pizza; we'll forgive them for that. The Sofia pizza is halfway there—good homemade mozzarella, past-their-prime "fresh" tomatoes. The no-cheese Rossa tomato pie could have used a more distinctive sauce; it's just there. But points for trying, and Rosario's is a colorful little neighborhood hangout.

Rose's Pizza, Penn Station, (212) 629–7455. This brightly-lit, charmless pizzeria is several steps from Caruso's, and no better. Be prepared to sweep the last user's crumbs and crumpled napkins from your table. The cheese on the plain slice looks dubious and tastes worse. The Grandma has an adequate burnt crust, but the sauce tastes not so much from the jar as from under it. If I were inebriated, I could almost eat it.

Rossetti's Pizza, 114 Sixth Avenue, (212) 966–7178. Red-neon "Pizza" sign in window, etching of the Brooklyn Bridge on mirrored wall, pizza boxes stacked nearly to the ceiling. Straightforward plain slice, with a blah crust; the seasoning separates it slightly from the pack.

Rubirosa Ristorante, 235 Mulberry Street, (212) 965–0500. Draw aside the curtain and follow your waitress to a series of ever-unfolding rooms. The soundtrack runs from 1950s girl groups to reggae. Owner Angelo Pappalardo's father, Giuseppe, is the Joe

FACT:
The world record for pizza eating: Patrick Bertoletti, who ate forty-seven slices of pizza in ten minutes.

behind the legendary Joe and Pat's on Staten Island. The margherita pizza is extra-thin (a New York rarity) and cracker-crusted. A small pizza here is big—thirteen inches—but it'll go quick because of its thinness. The tomato sauce is not as tart or distinctive as the one found in the excellent Grandma's braised beef braciole. Don't sleep on the pasta; the pappardelle, with sausage ragu and pecorino, is highly recommended.

Sacco Pizza, 819 Ninth Avenue, (212) 582–7765. Funky little pizza dive; on a busy night you don't say your order as much as shout it. Grandma pizza is on the menu, but they don't make it anymore. "No one wants it," moans the guy behind the counter. Poor Grandma. The plain cheese slice boasts an endearing burnt-cheese flavor, but not much else. The Sicilian is all cheese, no sauce, and nowhere. Maybe they should bring Grandma back.

Sal and Carmine's, 2671 Broadway, (212) 663–7651. Legendary neighborhood pizzeria. Great space—high ceilings and striking art; dig the poster of the half-naked Adonis with a towel strategically wrapped around him. Pizza served with a side of attitude, at least when we were there. Asked for a receipt, the sullen guy behind the counter replies, "I'd have to write it down." Well, gee whiz, you just go on and do that. The plain slice is cheesy to the max; the three tiny splotches of sauce made us wonder if a nationwide sauce rationing was in effect. The Sicilian is truly salty. My friend Kristin had the best line—"Tastes like pizza made at day camp."

Sal's Little Italy, 384 Broome Street, (212) 925–0440. Green-awninged, red-neon-lit storefront with photos of seemingly everyone who ever appeared on *The Sopranos* on the wall. Five stools in front; dining room in back. Slices available in plain only; there are individual and large pizzas, including the happily-titled Tutte le Carni (pomodoro sauce, mozzarella, pepperoni, sausage, and sliced meatball). Decent plain slice.

Sam's Famous Pizza, 150 East 116th Street, (212) 348–9437. If I were pizza mayor, the first thing I'd do is ban the use of the word "famous"; seemingly a quarter of the city's pizzerias have it in their name. I have no idea what's famous about Sam's; the crust is too chewy, the sauce indistinct. A huge slice is just $2.25, so that's something. The storefront, at the corner of Lexington and 116th Street, does have great curb appeal. The pizza boxes proclaim Sam's uses "the world's best ingredients." They can only wish.

San Matteo Panuozzo, 1739 Second Avenue, (212) 426–6943. Formerly known as San Matteo Pizza and Espresso Bar, this cozy space is a nice retreat from the Upper East Side blare and glare. The owners are Fabio Casella, who worked at Mike's Deli and Joe's Deli on Arthur Avenue in the Bronx, and Vincenzo Scardino, who built a gelateria in Italy and builds pizza ovens in this country. One menu novelty: panuozzo, a panini-like, honeycombed crust bread filled with pancetta, mortadella, chiodini mushrooms, and other ingredients. I liked the salsiccia e friarielli (mozzarella, sausage, broccoli rabe) pizza, didn't like the margherita, which managed to be floppy, soppy, and soft all at once.

Siena Pizza, 274 West 40th Street, (212) 391–9524. Two small leaning tables, three black stools, and a ledge, and steps—if you have long legs—from the Port Authority A, C, E subway stop. The slices don't look promising; the cheese has a faded-movie-star look, and the crust is close to tasteless, but it's pleasantly crunchy. The margherita fares better. The tart sauce is the best thing here; it belongs on a more worthy pizza.

SLICE, 535 Hudson Street, (212) 929–2920. Montreal-born, half-Japanese, half-Indian Miki Agrawal is the tireless owner of SLICE, which started on the Upper East Side in 2005 and is now in the West Village. The emphasis is on fresh, local, seasonal ingredients. The pizza is all over the ingredient map: There's the Miki (whole wheat crust, basil pesto, hormone-free chicken sausage, goat cheese, sun-dried tomatoes, fresh basil), the Bomb (herb crust, spicy free-range chicken tikka masala, mozzarella), and the Skilled Eggplant (herb crust, sun-dried tomato pesto, sautéed eggplant, kalamata olives, mozzarella). My favorite: the Guru, an herb-crusted pizza with marinara, sautéed mushrooms, goat cheese, free-range chicken sausage, and local fresh mozzarella. Maybe the city's priciest slices; several run $7 each.

Slice & Co., 527 Sixth Avenue, (212) 255–6333. Primo pizza location, at the corner of Sixth Avenue and 14th Street. Open-air in warmer months, with tin ceiling and exposed ductwork. "We've mastered the art of pizza making," a sign proclaims. Oh no you haven't. The Grandma uses decent tomatoes but a boring buttery assembly-line crust.

A Slice of New York, 727 Eighth Avenue, (212) 399–9555. Splendid orange-neon "Pizza" sign out front; inside it's a low-rent cafeteria look, and a surreal-looking upstairs dining room with seemingly half the city's fluorescent light on display. The white pizza, despite cheese that peels like sunburnt skin, is edible.

Solo Pizza, 27 Avenue B, (212) 420–7656. Three big tables, two smaller ones, and a classic rock soundtrack—"Freebird," "Brown-Eyed Girl," and so on. Peach-colored walls; photos of owner's children on them. Get a magnet with each purchase of a large pizza; collect eight magnets, get one large pizza free! Wanted to like the no-cheese focaccia, but despite the dash of oregano it lacks personality; the sauce is bland. The margherita boasts the same sauce, and the same results.

South Brooklyn Pizza, 122 First Avenue, (212) 533–2879. Probably the lowest-profile pizzeria in the city; there's no outdoor sign, just a red facade, with the business name written on a menu board inside. Baskets of onions and a seven-inch black-and-white General Electric TV add to the atmosphere, or lack of it.

Help yourself to peppers and extra-virgin olive oil. The margherita has unfortunate shredded cheese on top, but the sauce is good and distinctive. SBP is located next to Kim's Video and Music; if you don't know that, you may walk right past it. There is another Manhattan location on Bleecker Street, and Brooklyn stores in Carroll Gardens, Cobble Hill, North Slope, and South Slope.

Box for Stella's, Manhattan.

The no-name exterior of South Brooklyn Pizza, First Avenue, Manhattan.

Stella's Pizza, 110 Ninth Avenue, (212) 462–4444. Stella! A shoebox—or something smaller—of a place, several blocks from Port Authority, and with pizza markedly better than anything you'll find in the bus terminal. Five stools are lined up against a mirrored wall; a "Roy Lichtenstein Art of the Sixties" poster lends an improbable bit of design. Get the Sicilian, possibly the city's thickest, yet lighter-tasting than most. Really more bread than pizza, but good bread. If it had any sauce—good luck finding any—this would be a standout slice. The plain is pretty decent, somewhat more tomatoey than your usual New York slice.

Stromboli Pizza, 83 St. Marks Place, (212) 673–3691. Funky/fun decor—tin ceiling, chipped metal columns that look like they predate the Industrial Revolution, half a dozen tables, and an eating perch on a brick slab where spice containers are kept. Plus the city's most challenging-to-reach restroom; low overhang (watch your head!) and steep stairs lead to the basement. No wonder the guy behind the counter tells you to be careful before you start down. Intriguing selection of pizzas—the usual suspects, plus Grandmas, Grandpas, and focaccia. The plain is thin-crusted, extremely oily, and aggressively seasoned, with a faint smoky ting. The Grandpa is slightly better, despite the beat-up basil and cheese that looks like it's been spray-painted on.

Sullivan Street Bakery, 533 West 47th Street, (212) 265–5580. "The Mad Baker of Sullivan Street," read the headline of a *New York* magazine profile on Jim Leahy, the once-itinerant (in one year he held thirty-seven jobs) self-taught baker who opened his bakery in 1992 and Co. in 2009. The slices here are unlike any

Painted garbage can, Stromboli Pizza, Manhattan.

T&R Pizza, Amsterdam Avenue, Manhattan.

other—ultra-thin-crust creations that are more flatbread than pizza. Offerings include a bianca con pecorino, made with Sardinian sheep's milk pecorino, with breadcrumbs sprinkled on top; and a pizza funghi with crimini mushrooms, onions, thyme, olive oil, and sea salt. Small space—five wood-slatted chairs along a windowsill ledge.

T & R Pizza, 411 Amsterdam Avenue, (212) 787–4093. Red-neon-lit hole-in-the-wall, with three booths and four chairs. Another too-cheesy slice—check out the photo on their website; it'll either give you a heart attack or send you into gooey ecstasy. But the crust is crackery and distinctive. There's a white pizza loaded with black olives—always a good thing in my book—and decent tomatoes. Other pizzas include a marinara (no cheese), vegetarian (broccoli, eggplant, and mushrooms), and tomato and onion.

Times Square Pizzeria, 765 Eighth Avenue, (212) 245–1900. Located inside a Subway, so your hopes are not high from the start. And you don't get much, apart from bad spelling (one sign offers "pepproni," while the menu lists "the meat" as an

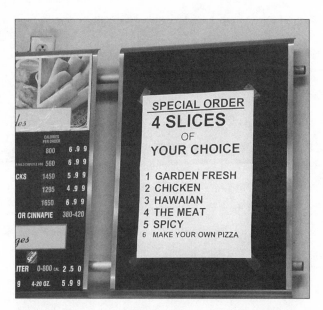

The Meat's on the menu at Times Square Pizzeria, Manhattan.

Misspelled sign, Times Square Pizzeria, Manhattan.

available topping). Times Square Pizza is certainly not at the crossroads of taste; the cheese on the plain tastes like rubber that melted in the sun, and the bottom looks like a tire tread. "Best Pizza in New York," proclaims the menu. It's the city's worst dollar slice.

Sign outside restroom door, Times Square Pizzeria.

Two Boots, Grand Central Station, lower dining concourse, (212) 557–7992. Two indie filmmakers with a love of all things New Orleans started the Cajun- and Creole-tinged Two Boots in 1987; the empire now includes eight stores in New York City and one each in Jersey City, Bridgeport, and Los Angeles. Toppings include the usual suspects, plus sopressata, crawfish, Creole chicken, and Cajun ham. The Grand Central Station location, across from Magnolia Bakery, may be the train station's hippest spot, a trippy mix of multicolored beads, 1960s psychedelia, and red banquettes. The Grandma Bess pizza is too heavy on the Parmigiano, but the organic San Marzano plum tomatoes, olive oil, and fresh basil more than make up for it. The Tony Clifton is an intriguing mix of wild mushrooms, sweet red pepper pesto, Vidalia onions, and mozzarella.

2 Bros. Pizza, 32 St. Marks Place; (212) 777–0600. The original location of the dollar-slice kingpin, and strategically located on one of the city's hippest streets. Hole-in-the-wall, at least up front; there's a narrow ledge for stand-up dining and a cafe-like area in back with squatty tables, perfect for kids, Munchkins, and adults who don't mind feeling squished. It's like being in some

Santas, part of the annual SantaCon festivities in New York, outside a 2 Bros. location.

Pizza pans await duty at 2 Bros. on St. Marks Place.

Alice in Wonderland pizza fantasy. One of the top three dollar slices in the city, with acceptable cheese and a semblance of sauce. A pepperoni or mushroom slice costs 50 cents extra.

Two N A Can Pizza, 1032 Sixth Avenue, (212) 398–3288. Another dollar-slice joint; original name, In-N-Out Pizza, was changed to avoid conflict with In-N-Out Burger. Brightly lit (pack your shades); no tables or chairs, but a long chrome ledge along a mirrored wall (check your pizza-eating technique, or makeup). If you can't grab a ledge spot, be prepared to lean against the wall. Somehow, it makes for a fun pizza experience, especially late at night. There's a hint of peppery flavor on the plain slice, but the usual way-too-soft crust makes it taste like a dozen other dollar slices, which makes you wonder if they came from the same central slice commissary.

Uncle Mario's Brick Oven Pizza, 739 Ninth Avenue, (212) 459–1234. Friendly Italian mama greets you, seats you, brings you water, even sings a little. When you grab your slice and produce money, she says, "Sit down, pay later." If only hundreds of other pizzeria owners in the city were half as friendly. She offers ground pepper, and you decline, but she brings it over anyway and insists it'll enhance the flavor, so you give in. The Grandma is ordinary, but the margherita features a spry, fresh-tasting sauce, with fresh basil, not the usual tired-looking leaves. Intriguing options: the puttanesca pizza, with capers, gaeta olives, roasted garlic, and olive oil, and the Uncle Mario's specialty pizza (sauce, arugula, prosciutto, shaved Parmesan).

Valducci's Pizza Truck, 52nd Street and Park Avenue, (212) 470–8476. Valducci's may serve the sauciest pizza in New York. Cheese? What's that? It's all California tomatoes, with a dusting of cheese. It's the "home of the super slice," and that's no lie; square slices run $3 to $5, but they're huge. Choices include a regular square, a Sicilian oreganata, a meatball and ricotta, and a white pizza, the last available as a whole pizza only. The square's flimsy crust needs work, but this is the city's best truck pizza, at least in the tomato pie category.

Villa Fresh Italian Kitchen, Port Authority Bus Terminal, (212) 971–9242. Intensely-lit cafeteria-like space; the Times Square location is located in what is decorously called the Market Food Court at Times Square. Stuffed pizza is the main attraction—signs advertise "stuff" vegetable and "stuff" meat pizzas. Dreadful pizzas—thick, subpar cheese, undercooked, and the sauce looks like it was crayoned on. One sign: "Made fresh daily since 1964." The photos of food on the wall are way more appetizing than anything served here.

Village Pizza, 65 Eighth Avenue, (212) 243–4367. "Thank you very much; enjoy, have a nice day," the friendly owner tells customers, even though he rarely smiles. Brick walls, cinder-block floors, several tables. Plenty of fans on Yelp, but apparently they don't get out much. The plain has an overcooked/burnt-cheese-and-sauce taste. The Grandma is plenty saucy and plenty average. For a better plain slice, hit Bleecker Street Pizza, about ten blocks away.

Vinny Vincenz, 231 First Avenue, (212) 674–0707. "Where old school meets gourmet," heralds the menu. White-tiled walls almost make you feel you're sitting inside a giant pizza oven. Or maybe my imagination

was just working overtime that day. Upside-down Luigi Vitelli peeled tomato cans hanging from ceiling. Mural on wall of four black-tied cigarette-smoking characters—gangsters? limo drivers? The plain is just fair, but the margherita is marvelous: plum tomatoes add a blast of flavor, and the crust is big and crispy. I kept dipping my fingers into the sauce; it's that good. The mozzarella could have been bubblier, but I'm nitpicking. Vinny's and Iggy's, several blocks away, know how to do sauce.

Vinny Vincenz, First Avenue, Manhattan.

West 190th Street Pizza, 1611 Saint Nicholas Avenue, (212) 923–4441. Yep, that's what it's called, and it's located right outside the 190th Street subway stop with its freight-elevator-only access. No-frills slice joint with no tables or chairs, but two orange-colored window ledges. Sign: "Let's be friends. No credit." The guy behind the counter gives me a slice from a whole hot pizza instead of the last slice from the one previous; thank you. The slice is put on wax paper, then slapped on the counter, oil seeping everywhere. Not a bad slice, considering.

Z Deli Pizzeria, 801–803 Eighth Avenue, (201) 315–1659. Dollar-slice joint. Same owners as Off Broadway Deli & Pizza, same dizzyingly expansive menu. Fresh is the word here. Fresh sandwiches! Fresh breakfast! Fresh dairy products! Fresh food daily! The pizza counter's in back. We have a winner in the dollar-slice Best Crust category: it's Z. Thick, browned, crispy: I could eat this crust all day. Maybe pizzerias should start offering just crust, the way bagel shops offer bagel chips? Oddly, it's not the same pizza you get at Off Broadway. Z's dollar slice is probably too oily, and the cheese looks as faded as the tile floor, but it's not boring and outdistances most of the competition. There are five tables in front; you may find yourself sitting next to a box of potatoes or a crate of red onions.

Zigolini's Pizza Bar, 675 Ninth Avenue, (212) 333–3900. Three flat screens above a long bar; seven tables by the window and more in back, where a brick oven is recessed in the wall. Bottles of wine racked on the wall look like torpedoes ready to be fired. Eclectic beer selection; you can't find Flying Dog Raging Bitch or Lagunitas Hop Stoopid Ale everywhere. The sausage on the Margherita Macellaio is one of the city's best; the pizza boasts the requisite charred crust and a slightly tart sauce. The Margherita Funghi marries first-rate mushrooms to another fine crust, but it's too oily/greasy for its own good.

FACT:
Carryout accounts for 36 percent of all pizzeria orders, while delivery accounts for 31 percent.

Queens

A & J Pizza & Restaurant, 71–37 Austin Street, Forest Hills, (718) 520–9018. Can't miss the big, bright green-and-red neon "Pizza" sign in the window. Menorahs and pizza men adorn the mirrored walls. Dig the salad pizza, with a jungle of greens, olives, and tomatoes on top. The plain slice, though, is oily and slightly rubbery-tasting. The Sicilian boasts a mildly pleasing crunch, but the cheese looks like it came through the forest, hills, and a few other things to get here. The focaccia approaches acceptability; there's a ton of tomato sauce, plus onions, garlic, and oregano.

Alba's Pizza & Restaurant, 36–20 Ditmars Boulevard, Astoria, (718) 932–5924. Pizzeria/restaurant/bar, and busy in the evening. Not-so-ordinary beers on tap include Peak Organic IPA. Two slices and a craft beer for about $10? Sign me up. The fresh mozzarella and marinara slice didn't take well to reheating, or maybe it wasn't so fresh to begin with. The Grandma is one you may not welcome into your family—overly cheesy, a mere oval of red sauce in the middle, and exhausted-looking basil.

Amore Pizza, 3027 Stratton Street, Flushing, (718) 445–0579. Squeezed into a strip mall along with Dunkin' Donuts, a Chinese restaurant, a liquor store, and a 24-hour check cashing service, with planes from LaGuardia booming overhead. Packed on a Saturday night, and I'm not sure why. The plain: cheap-crackly crust and mushy, gushy cheese. The Sicilian: chewy, pasty. Both are undercooked. One table is littered with beer bottles. Ah, maybe that's the secret to enjoying it.

Ariana's Pizzeria & Restaurant, 70–32 Austin Street, Forest Hills, (718) 263–3094. Check for daily pizza specials; there was an artichoke pizza the day I visited. The plain is better than nearby A & J's, but that's no ringing endorsement. The margherita looked like the best of the dozen slices on display, and it's halfway to happy. The painfully thin, brittle crust is nearly rescued by the blob of olive-oil-topped runny mozzarella and a solid sauce.

Bella Via Bar & Restaurant, 47–46 Vernon Boulevard, Long Island City, (718) 361–7510. Italian restaurant with large dining room, subdued lighting; whole pizzas only. The margherita looked like a model pizza but proved something less: good-enough cheese, but a so-so sauce and too-soft/chewy crust and bottom. Needed more time in the oven; more attention, period.

Boston Pizza, 37–02 Broadway, Astoria, (718) 545–6001. Small quarters and sagging ceiling; you can also get cheese rolls and empanadas. Want to know what a grilled cheese pizza tastes like? Try the pan pizza here; the result is not disagreeable, texture-wise, with a light crisp crust, but it tastes bland.

Da Franco Ristorante Italiano & Brick Oven Pizza, 23–92 21st Street, Astoria, (718) 267–0010. Sandwiched between a Thai restaurant and a Thai spa, Da Franco opened in 2009; owner Franco Spatola also owns Forno Italia in Astoria. Mozzarella for both is made at a Ridgewood, New York, factory he co-owns. No slices. Call the margherita a beginner's version—perfectly acceptable, but there's barely any sauce, and the crust doesn't taste fully formed, or cooked.

Dee's, 107–23 Metropolitan Avenue, Forest Hills, (718) 793–7553. Retro-stylish; looks more like a swanky

FACT:
According to *The Dictionary of Italian Food and Drink,* the word "pizza" first surfaced around A.D. 1000 as "picea" or "piza," from pizzicare, "to pluck," most likely a reference to the way cooks had to yank the hot pie from the oven.

1950s airport lounge than pizzeria. Menu is expansive: organic carrot and ginger soup, Australian lamb chops, Mom's meatloaf, and more. Earn one point for every dollar spent in the Frequent Dining Club; 10,000 points earns you a dinner party for five! The margherita joins good cheese and sauce, although there's not much of the latter. And it's too soft and spongy underneath. A good-looking but not especially well executed margherita.

Elegante Restaurant & Pizzeria, 92–01 Rockaway Beach Boulevard, Rockaway Beach, (718) 634–3914. The A train ride to Beach 90th Street is unsurpassingly cool, the train bouncing past Aqueduct Racetrack and JFK International Airport, then seeming to skim over the waters of Jamaica Bay. Wish the pizza at Elegante were as thrilling. Lively crew of guys behind counter; the talk is of football, girls, and life, in roughly that order. The plain slice is oily/greasy, and the decent crisp is marred by a pasty, flimsy-crackery crust. The marinara is supposed to be the standout slice here. It looks like a mistake—the sauce is a deep blood-red—but it tastes somewhat better. The boatload of garlic and oregano may be the best thing going for it.

Frankie's Pizza, 22–56 31st Street, Astoria, (718) 956–9525. "The best pizzeria in Astoria for almost 50 years," crows the menu, which also advertises "special" subs, "delicious" pasta, "famous" slices, and "gourmet" pizza. The plain slice, alas, is famously mediocre. The Sicilian boasts a nice bready bottom, but the cheese is browned and dubious-looking, and it's not because of the lighting.

Gino's Pizzeria & Restaurant, 158–46 Cross Bay Boulevard, Howard Beach, (718) 738–4113. Several blocks from the heralded New Park Pizza, and, heresy or not, better. Spacious brick-walled restaurant; take your slice to one of the cavernous booths. The plain is crispy, oily, with a slightly burnt top. Solid slice. The squares here come in straight Sicilian, marinara, and one with fresh mozzarella and basil, the last a standout. A lovely sweet sauce and above-average crust add up to one of the better Sicilians in the city.

Joey's Pizzeria, 69–07 Grand Avenue, Maspeth, (718) 779–5880. Brightly lit, with red/green neon tubing rampant, and orange booths. "How are you doing, Mr. Dino?" a counter guy greets a regular. "How's everything? Working hard?" They love their red sauce here; there are imposing clumps of tomatoes atop the Grandma, which is thicker and more substantial than most. The crust can't make up its mind whether it wants to be chewy or crispy. But you've got to admire the bounty of tomatoes. "What do you want to drink?" a guy in a corner booth asks his girlfriend. "Alcohol," she says. "Not yet," he replies.

John's Pizzeria, 85–02 Grand Avenue, Elmhurst, (718) 457–7561. Classic slice joint, and maybe the city's only pizzeria run by a mother-and-daughter team.

John's opened in 1965 on the next block over, moving to its current location, a drugstore, in 1976. Lively neighborhood hangout, with schoolkids and cops among the faithful. No bills over $20 accepted, and no restrooms. The plain pizza is classic New York style—nothing dramatic or life-changing, just a good honest slice.

La Villa Pizzeria, 8207 153rd Avenue, Howard Beach, (718) 641–8259. Diner-like counter in front shares space with wood-fired brick ovens; dining room in back. Many of the pizzas are available as regular round, deep-dish round, or square. The focaccia della Nonna translates as "Grandma's Pizza," but it's not a traditional Grandma slice, at least not in round or deep-dish form. The cheese and bread are better than those on its Sicilian cousin at L&B Spumoni, but the plum tomatoes could have been fresher, or spryer. The margherita round would have made Queen Margherita happy, with its assertive sauce, slightly burnt edges and fine, chewy crust. It's easily one of the best pizzas in Queens.

Box, La Villa Pizzeria, Queens.

La Vita Mia Pizza & Grill Restaurant, 28–01 24th Avenue, Astoria, (718) 267–0310. "If you smoke," reads a sign here, "leave your butt outside." Go for the Philly cheesesteak pizza and pineapple pizza if it's, like, your last day on earth. The best-seller is the Grandma, with mozzarella, organic tomato sauce, and a touch of garlic. It's different; I couldn't decide whether I liked it or not. The three-cheese (mozzarella, ricotta, and Parmesan) is huge, but judging by the result, they might have done better sticking to one cheese; that trio just doesn't seem to work well together, or at least here.

Lillian Pizzeria, 96–01 69th Avenue, Forest Hills, (718) 520-8749. Pleasant, clean pizzeria with orange neon sign, open since 1971. The plain slice is seriously oily but satisfying. The Sicilian featured a faint lemony tinge, not odd, just different, and in any event nothing special.

Lorusso Gourmet Pizza Focaccia, 18–01 26th Road, Astoria, (718) 777–3628. Cute corner spot in residential neighborhood; imported olive oil and cookies lend it a small market look. There are plain, margherita, Sicilian, white, and other pizzas on the menu, but the house specialty is the pizza focaccia—round four-slice mini pizzas. About a dozen are on display. The fresh mozzarella and roasted peppers is a winning combo.

Maspeth Pizza, 71–09 Grand Avenue, Maspeth, (718) 639–5050. Brightly lit, clean tile floors, "chicken soup" and "pasta fagioli" written in multicolored marker on paper plates taped to wall. Pretty much everything that could go wrong with a focaccia goes wrong here: off-color cheese; off-putting sauce; uncooked core. No amount of garlic and oregano could hide it. Keep walking . . . to Rose's.

FACT:
Monster Fly Trap, which sells its "earth friendly" items to pizzerias and other restaurants, claims to have killed more than 20 million flies over the years.

Mazara Pizzeria & Restaurant, 105–03 Metropolitan Avenue, Forest Hills, (718) 544–0416. "As seen in *Forest Hills Celebrity & Entertainment Magazine,*" announces a sign. The mural here—sun-washed villas, sailboats, waterfront cafe, blue sky—makes my list of top ten pizzeria murals in the city. The plain is nearly devoid of sauce; must have taken the LIRR out of town. The fresh mozzarella, meanwhile, is without sauce or basil, but it's a winner; the homemade pesto enlivens an already-distinctive slice, the oil running off in rivulets for extra effect. The best slice, with Gino's in Howard Beach, on the first of several all-day Queens trips.

Michael Angelo's II Pizzeria & Restaurant, 29–11 23rd Avenue, Astoria, (718) 932–2096. You've got to like a place where slices are served on real plates, or at least they were on a midafternoon visit. White tablecloths, and nubile nymphs on the walls. Huge, cheesy slices; good luck finding sauce. Bready, crunchy, fun crust. Size is the only thing going for the margherita; the cheese looked a bit outdated.

Neighborhood Pizzeria & Restaurant, 4 Coleman Square, Old Howard Beach, (718) 641–7520. Right across the street from the Howard Beach A train stop.

Pizza wall decor is usually from hunger; here's one that stands out: a framed collection of dollar bills from scores of countries—Paraguay, Uruguay, Guyana, Chile, and more. Hey, when you're eating one mediocre slice after another, you need something to take your mind off things. The plain slice is wan-looking, but I liked the soft, bready crust. The Grandma is closer to a Sicilian, with its thick, bready core and a thin landing strip or two of sauce. Not bad, and probably better than anything you'll find in the airport.

New Park Pizza, 156–71 Cross Bay Boulevard, Howard Beach, (718) 641–3082. Should be on any NYC pizza lover's itinerary. You can eat in the rear dining room, but for max effect sit down at one of the four picnic benches in front—they tilt seriously to one side. Sign above counter: "Parents. Please Do Not Leave Children Alone on Benches. They May Lean Back and Fall." The pizza could get to them, too. The Sicilian's kind of a mess, with the cheese fractured on top like fissures on Mars, and the sauce is borderline bad. The plain is a slight step up, but it's too floppy and the crust

Parental advisory, New Park Pizza, Howard Beach.

too doughy. Pizza for, well, children. Legions of admirers, but you go to New Park for the scene, not the pizza.

Nick's Pizza, 108–26 Ascan Avenue, Forest Hills, (718) 263–1126. Queens landmark is more bistro than pizzeria, with hardwood floors, high ceilings, exposed ductwork, a massive white column in the middle of the room, and animated conversation. Cash only, and no slices. There are no set pizzas; choose regular or white, and add toppings of choice, everything from sausage, mushrooms, and olives to feta, scallions, and prosciutto. Can't decide? Go with the half white, half red, like I did. The former features a good, tangy sauce, the latter

The famous New Park Pizza, Howard Beach.

dreamy-creamy ricotta. Wish both had been crispier, but overall better than Dee's. Owner Nick Angelis also co-owns Adrienne's Pizzabar and Harry's Italian Pizza Bar in Manhattan.

Rizzo's Fine Pizza, 30–13 Steinway Street, Astoria, (718) 721–9862. Iconic Queens pizzeria opened in 1959 by brothers Joseph and Salvatore Rizzo and brother-in-law Hugo Lupi. "It's hip to be square" is the slogan, a reference to the thin-crust Sicilian. It's good and saucy, with a nearly cracker crust. The plain is similarly saucy, but otherwise nothing special. The margherita is loaded

Rizzo's Pizza, Queens.

with oregano, but the seasoning couldn't disguise the overall lack of flavor. At Rizzo's, go square or don't go at all.

Rosario's Deli, 22–55 31st Street, Astoria, (718) 728–2920. An imported pasta lover's vision of paradise; floor-to-ceiling shelves are stocked with pastas and sauces. Boxes of panettone suspended from the ceiling make it appear like it's raining loaves of sweet bread. With all the pasta, deli meats, candies, and items like "all-natural muscle brownies," it's easy to miss the pizza; a whole pie is practically hidden from view behind the counter. It's a crispy, oily, crunchy plain slice, with cheese and sauce in sweet balance. A grandfatherly type sits on a chair in the middle of the action, greeting customers. Love this place.

Rosario's Famous La Bella Pizza & Pasta, 38–01 Ditmars Boulevard, Astoria, (718) 626–2660. No connection to Rosario's Deli. "We are the best!" the menu modestly proclaims. Opened in 2010, and it's famous . . . somewhere. The Sicilian is built well enough; there's only one problem—there's zero seasoning and close to zero taste. Creative choices, anyway: a formaggia marinara pizza with ricotta, mozzarella, minced garlic, and plum tomatoes; and La Puttanesca Pizza with minced green and black olives, capers, onions, mozzarella, anchovy, and plum tomatoes.

Rose & Joe's Italian Bakery, 22–40 31st Street, Astoria, (718) 721-9422. Located on the other side of the elevated tracks from Rosario's Deli, this smallish bakery offers bread, cookies, pastries, pies, biscotti—and pizza, available at a counter in back. There are no tables, so you may have to take that slice out on the sidewalk and chow down to the rumble of subway trains. Slices are thoughtfully wrapped in foil instead of just being crammed in a bag. I'm not a fan of the margherita's buttery, crackery crust; you may be. The sauce—nice. The square is an oily, tasty treat, but practically all cheese.

Rose & Joe's, Queens.

Rose's Pizza, 55–26 69th Street, Maspeth, (718) 446–5910. Housed in an imposing four-story red-neon-lit warehouse-looking building. The interior is all Queens diner. Copies of the *Italian-American Journal* on a windowsill. I often chose slices by what looked best. The margherita here looked promising, and it delivered. It's an immense slice, and immensely satisfying, the cheese running like a valley through two red hills of sauce, the crust extra-chewy. But my eyes failed me with the second most-promising-looking slice, the white. There's a layer of uncooked dough. One strike. So-so cheese. Two strikes. I didn't wait for a third.

Sac's Place, 25–41 Broadway, Astoria, (718) 204–5002. Celebrated Queens pizzeria with "world renowned" coal-oven pizza. Sculpture of ironworkers perched on girder is a step up from the usual pizzeria kitsch. The marinara,

a cheeseless square with fresh tomatoes, basil, garlic, and extra-virgin olive oil, is somewhere between a Grandma and a Sicilian; love the red sauce. The plain, with the same winning sauce, may be too floppy for some, but get over it; good cheese and crust add up to a first-rate slice.

Sandro's Pizza, 24–17 Ditmars Boulevard, Astoria, (718) 777–1700. I dig holes-in-the-wall, but this is one HITW you may want to avoid, unless you're a schoolkid, and then it may somehow entice. The plain slice is gummy and yucky; it's worse than even Penn Station pizza, which is saying something. There is a "Famous" Cleaners business just down the street; good thing Sandro's makes no such claim.

Steinway Pizza, 31–51 Steinway Street, Astoria, (718) 274–4250. Statue of the Blessed Virgin atop a refrigerator, along with the American and Mexican flags. The white pizza looked promising but turned out to be little more than cheese on bread, neither especially memorable. The Sicilian is much better; the sauce tasted like Ragu, but I liked the sturdy, chewy crust.

Zack's Pizzeria/Papo Fried Chicken, 48–11 Vernon Boulevard, Long Island City, (718) 707–0332. It's never a good sign when a pizzeria offers pizza, fried chicken, spaghetti, fish and chips, and ice cream. Even less so when a sign advertising the ten-piece chicken special announces it's "leg and Thai" only. The pan pizza is a novelty; doesn't mean you'd want to put it in your mouth. Unformed, baby crust, zero crunch. Save your two-plus bucks.

Staten Island

Brother's Pizza, 750 Port Richmond Avenue, (718) 442–2332. Busy corner, where Port Richmond Avenue, Forest Avenue, and Willowbroook Road meet in the shadow of the West Shore Expressway. The Sicilian is soft, chewy, gooey, and screamingly ordinary. The plain is greasy/oily but quite pleasing; the cheese works better here than on the Sicilian. The Grandma slice is better than both.

Cafe Milano Pizzeria & Restaurant, 401 Forest Avenue, (718) 720–1313. Restaurant to one side; takeout, with four tables, on the other. Friendly, almost jovial staff. Sweet little Grandma, brimming with good sauce and cheese. Even better: the mozzarella pizza with basil and tomato. A bit watery on top, and the tomatoes could have been fresher, but the cheese, sauce, and crust are excellent.

Ciro Pizza Cafe, 862 Huguenot Avenue, (718) 605–0620. Across the street from the Huguenot train station, and good luck squeezing into the tiny parking lot. There's exactly one chair on the takeout side; a dining room is on the other side of a brown curtain. The plain slice, thin-crusted and tomatoey, is one of the two or three best on the island. The Sicilian, with a halfway-to-burnt crust, is nice and tomatoey. "Gourmet" pizzas include one with arugula, cherry tomatoes, fresh mozzarella, and prosciutto, and a white ricotta pizza with marinated artichokes.

Cousin's Pizza, 4553 Arthur Kill Road, (718) 227–1805. Staten Island definitely has the best pizzeria murals. The one here, on both walls, shows the Cousin's storefront on one side of a canal with swift-flowing blue water; the effect is Venice comes to Staten Island, or vice versa. The plain slice is decent; much better is the one with fresh mozzarella and a lively, fresh-tasting marinara sauce.

Denino's Pizzeria & Tavern, 524 Port Richmond Avenue, (718) 442–9401. Only Staten Island location of this legendary pizzeria, opened in 1937; a sister location opened in Brick, New Jersey, in 2010. Classic, crispy thin-crust, with a slightly puffy, burnt-at-the-edges crust, and the sauce and cheese spread evenly. The family added a margherita pizza two years ago after much sampling; they've never offered a Sicilian pizza. No credit cards, no delivery, just old-school goodness.

Frank and Danny's, 4369 Amboy Road, (718) 317–1100. Open two years in the former Valducci's location, Frank and Danny's offers "our family's secret recipes." Yeah, you and about a hundred other pizzerias around the city. The "L&B Style Sicilian" is several subway stops shy of the one at the legendary Gravesend pizzeria; it's more tomatoey than the original, but there's an unfortunate uncooked gum line. The fresh mozzarella and tomato slice, apparently not modeled after anyone's, is better. Six kinds of Sicilians here, including a three-cheese garlic variety. Unlikely touch: The beer taps sit next to the fax machine.

Joe & Pat's, 1758 Victory Boulevard, (718) 981–0887. Owner Giuseppe Pappalardo worked at Ciro's, Nunzio's, and Tokie's before opening Joe & Pat's in 1960. His son, A.J., opened Rubirosa in Nolita in 2010. Both use a family recipe for the thin-crust pizza, thinner even than Lee's. But it doesn't quite have the same crisp as Lee's, and the so-so curl sausage is not in the same league.

True thin-crust is hard to find in the city, though, so Joe & Pat's will satisfy those types of longings. Plenty of pizza choices, including clams, red or white ricotta, prosciutto, pesto, whole wheat, and a heart-shaped pizza "for special occasions."

Justino's Pizzeria & Restaurant, 89 Guyon Avenue, (718) 668–2020. "Love at first slice" is the motto here. Exactly four celeb photos on the wall—Sinatra, Monroe, Pacino, and Presley. Who else do you need? Sign on menu: "Student special. Free fountain soda with any 2 SLS. Wow!" The Grandma boasts a bright tomato sauce, but the crust seemed lost and a bit bland. The fresh mozzarella and shredded cheese slice, though, is a winner: Puffy browned cheese bubbles and a tart sauce will have you hooked at first bite.

Lee's Tavern, 60 Hancock Street, (718) 667–9749. So this is where the boys are; a weekday afternoon visit revealed an all-guy packed house. No sign outside saying "Lee's"; look for the neon beer signs in the window. Bustling bar and tables in front, brick-walled dining room in back, TV screens of various sizes everywhere. Two mounted deer heads round out the decor. Staten Island—make that New York—is not exactly known as the home of true thin-crust, but that's what Lee's does, and does really well. I wanted to devour my half plain, half sausage on the spot—actually in my car. An airy, crackly crust and distinctive sauce make for a first-rate pizza. Excellent sausage. Whole pies and bar pies only; no slices.

Mona Lisa Pizzeria & Restaurant, 839 Annadale Road, (718) 967–1000. Predictable photo of you-know-who on the menu; the surprise here is the variety of square slices, a half dozen or more. There's a vodka, an "L&B," a "New York" (sauce and grated cheese), and a "gold medal–winning" mushroom and truffles. Grandpa pizzas (a thin-crust Sicilian like a Grandma but with the cheese, not sauce, on top) are rare in the city, and this one's recommended, although you'd better like garlic. The "old-fashioned" slice marries mozzarella and perky little tomatoes with a thin, crispy, slightly buttery-tasting crust.

Nucci's South Italian Restaurant & Pizzeria, 4842 Arthur Kill Road, (718) 967–3600. The fun's out in the parking lot; a mural, half obscured by a fence, shows two hands nearly touching à la Michelangelo's Sistine Chapel, along with male angels swooping in with salt and pepper shakers, a raven-haired beauty bearing a bottle of wine, and tomatoes and meatballs falling from the sky. The artist is Geoff Rawling, and the piece is part of the NYCArtsCypher program. Inside, to the left, is a small takeout area; to the right, a huge, handsome dining room. Whole pizzas only. A half plain, half sausage proved pleasing, a thin-crust pizza with a bit of give in the crust and quality chunk sausage.

Nunzio's Pizzeria & Restaurant, 2155 Hylan Boulevard, (718) 667–9647. Opened in 1942; check out the vintage photos and postcards on the wall, including one titled "Jack's Day Out, Lexington Avenue, 1912." No tables on the takeout side, just a long high counter that will come up to your chin if you're short, or a kid. The plain slice is built just right: crackly crust, good cheese, fun little sauce. The Sicilian boasts a pleasant burnt crust, but the cheese overwhelms everything; wish there were more than a trace of sauce.

Pier 76 Italian Restaurant, 76 Bay Street, (718) 447–7437. Maybe my favorite "pizza bar" in the city. The deep red awning and painted American flag on the facade remind me of a boardwalk stand. Inside are funky tasseled burgundy curtains, hi-def TV screens, a dartboard, red-checked-tablecloth tables in back, and a trophy case with a massive gold belt commemorating the "Tequila Fantasy Football League World Wrestling Champion," whoever or whatever that is. Good thin-crust pizza with a pebbly foundation, and sauce you can taste. Skip the sausage; you've been there, done that. Great place to spend a rainy day.

Salvatore of Soho, 1880 Hylan Boulevard, (718) 979–7499. Salvatore Ganci, a former pizza man at Lombardi's, claims his strip mall pizzeria boasts Staten Island's "only coal-fired brick oven." Smallish place, with five tables on each side. The clam pizza features the

FACT:
There are 65,000-plus pizza stores in the United States. The top fifty pizza chains own 43 percent of the pizzerias and control 52 percent of sales.

biggest clams I've seen anywhere; they're 1950s-mutant-monster-sized. The pizza itself: chewy crust, little crunch or char. The Neapolitan could have used more seasoning, but it was probably the best single slice during my initial Staten Island pizza excursion.

The Square, 1910 Hylan Boulevard, (718) 979–4700. Small place—five tables—with tiny parking lot; you may end up parking well down the residential side street. "The place of the great square pie," the menu proclaims. It's got a ways to go to reach great. The cheese takes a back seat to the sauce, which is good, and the bread has more crunch and flavor than most, with a nicely blackened bottom, but there's an unfortunate, and sizeable, uncooked layer.

Tony's Brick Oven, 1140 Bay Street, (718) 816–6516. Strip mall pizzeria; look for the blue neon coffee cup and red neon "Pizza" sign. Copies of *La Repubblica* and the *Daily News* are spread on a table. The spacious dining room includes a less-than-flattering mural of Tony; then again, I never met Tony. Average Sicilian—way too cheesy—but the margherita is one of the thickest anywhere, with credible cheese and a just-burnt-enough crust.

Trattoria Romana, 1476 Hylan Boulevard, (718) 980–3113. Waiters in crisp white shirts, but the kind of restaurant made for a family gathering or baby shower. You practically walk into the smallish bar just inside the entrance. If you want to order takeout, see the hostess at the Wizard of Oz–like curtained booth to the left. Excellent pizzas—the funghi with its quality mushrooms, the salsiccia with top-notch sausage. It's a drippy, oozing pizza, with a slightly blackened crust, and highly recommended.

Village Maria Pizzeria and Sidewalk Cafe,
3995 Amboy Road, (718) 984–2502. Another daft
mural; the one here shows a girl stealing pasta from the
owner's plate, and wild-eyed waiters ready to swoop on
the table. Novel choices include pan pizza; a stuffed
mozzarella with fresh basil; and a chicken française,
complete with lemon. The fresh mozzarella and tomato
had just two dainty dollops of sauce, and the latter
wasn't to my liking. But the pan pizza is a thick, chunky
delight, with soft, bready crust and crunchy top; it's a
nice combo of contrasting pizza textures.

Villa Monte Restaurant & Pizzeria, 2811 Richmond
Avenue, (718) 494–6554. This place could hold a
wedding or two, with two dining rooms and a bar. The
owner must love the horses; photos of Thoroughbreds
outnumber those of Yankees players. Probably the biggest
stack of pizza boxes anywhere; I stopped counting at five
hundred. You can never have enough pizza boxes. Good
Grandma, with a tart sauce and a snap/crackly crust. The
bruschetta is loaded with a garden's worth of tomatoes
but didn't quite come out as hoped.

Index

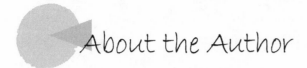

About the Author

Peter Genovese is a feature writer for the Newark *Star-Ledger*. He has written ten books, including *Roadside Jersey, Jersey Diners, The Great American Road Trip: US 1, Maine to Florida,* and *The Jersey Shore Uncovered: A Revealing Season on the Beach* for Rutgers University Press; *Roadside Florida* for Stackpole Books; *The Food Lover's Guide to New Jersey* and *New Jersey Curiosities* for Globe Pequot Press; and *Jersey Eats* and *A Slice of Jersey* for Pediment Publishing.